W9-BZZ-975

How The West was Won

THE
MOUNTAIN MEN

BILL HARRIS

Skyhorse Publishing

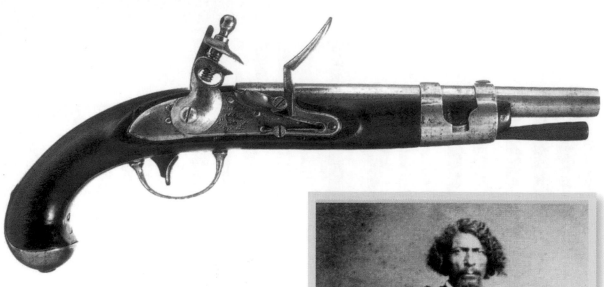

Skyhorse Publishing books may be purchased in bulk at
special discounts for sales promotion, corporate gifts,
fund-raising, or educational purposes. Special editions can
also be created to specifications. For details, contact the
Special Sales Department, Skyhorse Publishing,
307 West 36th Street, 11th Floor, New York, NY 10018 or
"mailto:info@skyhorsepublishing.com"info@skyhorsepublishing.com.

Skyhorse® and Skyhorse Publishing® are registered
trademarks of Skyhorse Publishing, Inc.®,
a Delaware corporation.

www.skyhorsepublishing.com

10 9 8 7 6 5 4 3 2 1

Library of Congress Cataloging-in-Publication Data TK

ISBN: 9781616086169

Printed in China

Contents

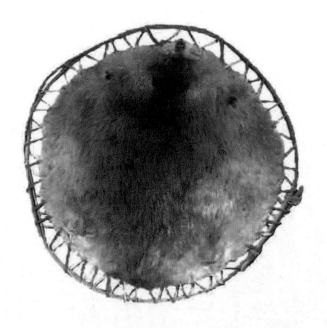

Introduction

The popular legends of the mountain men were generated over a surprisingly short period of time in America's history. Fewer than forty years had passed between their earliest forays up the Missouri River in the early 1800s and the final Rendezvous at Horse Creek in 1840. The mountain men legends were based on harrowing tales of survival against incredible odds. Harsh winter conditions, dangerous terrain, and the constant threat of Indian encounters all challenged even the hardiest of the mountain men. Some stories, like that of John Colter, who is thought to have been the first white man to have explored what is now Yellowstone National Park, were derided as being far-fetched. In order to survive, a mountain man had to be a superb marksman, a skilled horseman and trapper, and intimately familiar with nature and the seasons. As they sought ever more distant trapping grounds, the mountain men carved out a path than made the crossing of the American continent a reality rather than a dream.

The Mountain Men is designed to be a detailed chronicle of the lives of an extraordinarily rugged and resourceful breed of men. It draws on every aspect of their lives to create an accurate picture of what it meant to be one of these consummate outdoorsmen. From their earliest days as engages, or greenhorns, the mountain men worked hard and lived a substantially outdoor life, whatever the weather. It was only after proving their determination and hardiness that these young men could graduate to setting traps. Their ambition was to become a full-fledged trapper, with company-supplied traps and equipment. Their efforts resulted in a booming fur industry. Around $300,000 worth of pelts were shipped from St. Louis, Missouri, every year during the heyday of the trade. Some of the greatest fortunes in America, like that of the Astor family, were founded in the fur business. The founder of the American Fur Company, John Jacob Astor, became one of the richest men on the continent. When the beaver trade was finished, the seventy-year-old Astor (who had used his profits to buy up Manhattan farmland) became known as "the landlord of New York."

Sporting a highly distinctive kit, the mountain man became a highly recognizable character in the West. Dressed largely in materials he found in nature, his costume of skin and fur enabled him to blend perfectly into the virgin terrain.

The mountain men were heavily influenced by the Native Americans, who they also feared and competed with. Many carried steel tomahawks on their saddles and

Opposite page : Rocky Mountains, Colorado.

Below : A typical mountain man knife

Opposite page: Joe Grandee's Painting 'The Mountain Man' shows in realistic detail the buckskin jacket, beaver skin hat, muzzle loading rifle, and horn handled butcher knife that so typified the garb of the time.

favored the guns that the Indians also preferred. They were also equally dependant on their horses. Their style of dress was heavily influenced by the tribes, too; hide moccasins were standard mountain man garb, for example. Like the native inhabitants of the region, the mountain men knew that their success and survival depended on an intimate understanding of the natural world, its wildlife, weather, and terrain.

This book also commemorates some of the legendary characters that spent at least part of their amazing lives as mountain men. These include the celebrated free trapper and explorer Jim Bridger, who discovered the South Pass, a twenty-mile gap in the Continental Divide that became the route of the Oregon Trail. Hugh Glass was another famous outdoorsman. When he and his partner were captured by Pawnees, and his unfortunate partner slow-roasted to death over an open fire, Glass's extreme bravery in the face of death encouraged the Indians to spare his life, and adopt him as a blood brother. Jim Beckwourth was another extraordinary character from the mountain man mold. Beckwourth had an amazing capacity for cooperation with the Indian tribes, even the hostile Blackfoot and Crow. General Ashley highly valued him as an emissary to the Indians. Jim ended up with nine Indian wives, and when he died, the Crow gave him a chief's funeral. Bill Sublette was another highly important mountain man explorer who became a gentleman-adventurer. He tamed the Rocky Mountain passes and blazed the trail for the countless thousands of emigrants that would follow.

By the time of the final Rendezvous in 1840, the mountain men had left an indelible mark on the Western landscape. On the one hand, the beaver population had all but collapsed; the animals had been hunted to near-extinction and made into a huge range of hats, from tricorners to Stetsons. On the other hand, the trappers had pretty much mapped the West by this time, and the ways to get there. The mountain passes they discovered and the wagon routes they opened up were to prove a huge stimulus to western expansion, and led to a massive population shift to the new territories of the West.

Apart from their legend, this is undoubtedly the lasting legacy of the American mountain men. The demand for beaver fur has long since died out, but the tracks of the mountain men are still there to be seen.

Men to Match the Mountains

The Plains Indians called the Rockies the Shining Mountains, and in her anthem America the Beautiful, Katharine Lee Bates described them as "purple mountain majesties above the fruited plain." They still do shine across the prairies and, yes, they are quite possibly the most majestic mountains on earth.

The Rockies aren't the world's highest mountains by a long shot, but only the South American Andes stretch a greater distance. Even the rugged Himalayas don't cover as much territory as the North American Rockies, which run for more than three thousand miles northward from New Mexico and across Canada into Alaska, by way of Utah, Colorado and Idaho, Wyoming and Montana. Like all mountain chains, they are broken into individual ranges, more than a hundred of them in this case, with wide watershed basins and valleys between them. As many as twenty substantial rivers and thousands of creeks and streams run through the Rockies on their way to ultimately drain into three different oceans: the Atlantic, the Pacific, and the Arctic, not to mention the Gulf of Mexico; whether they flow east, west, north or south depends on their location in relation to the Continental Divide that runs along the crests of the mountains' highest ridges.

Thanks to a string of American and Canadian National Parks, and mile after mile of protected forests and wildlife reserves, the landscape of the Rocky Mountains haven't changed much since it first awed the Native Americans and later visitors like K. L. Bates, who found mountain majesty at the top of Pike's Peak in Colorado.

Hundreds of thousands of people go into these mountains every year for skiing and fly-fishing, hiking, rock climbing, hunting, or simply restoring their souls in the midst of the most beautiful surroundings in the world, but relatively few actually live there. The population density is less than five persons per square mile, and most of those people live in cities that are small compared to the American average. When Americans began turning their eyes to the West at the end of the eighteenth century, they couldn't see beyond the walls of the Rockies. But the barriers eventually came down thanks to a band of men— each part adventurer, part explorer, part Indian fighter, and part fur trapper— who risked their lives up there in the high mountains, deep canyons, and broad windswept meadows. It was a new breed of American, called the mountain men.

Above: Katharine Lee Bates visited the Rockies (opposite page) in summer 1893 when she attended a teaching workshop in Colorado Springs. Her observations were encapsulated in the words of her famous anthem, "America the Beautiful".

Between the years 1807 and 1840, when fur trading dominated in the Rockies, thousands of these men came and went, and each of them made his own personal contribution to the mountain man legend. Only a relative handful of their individual stories have survived, but each and every one of them was a textbook example of what are sometimes called rugged individualists who defy pigeonholing. Still, there were some qualities that most of them had in common.

More often than not a mountain trapper was a man in his twenties or thirties who had come from the South or the Midwest, or from farms up in Canada. Nearly all of them had spent their boyhoods on farms, in fact, and volunteers from the urban Northeast were nearly nonexistent. Even though the fur companies they worked for preferred to hire bachelors, a surprising majority of them were married men, although they left their wives behind when they went into the wilderness like soldiers marching off to war. Quite a few who went into the mountains as single men (not to mention many who already had wives at home) acquired Indian women who cooked for them, made and mended their clothes, and sometimes served as guides, not to mention providing companionship during weeks and months of virtual solitude. These kinds of arrangements were easily made with the women's fathers or brothers, who were usually more than willing to swap them for a gun or a horse. Although these women were never regarded as wives in the world of the white man, the mountain men themselves frequently saw them as "till death do us

Right: Most of the recruits–or engagés–as they were called, came from farming communities in the Midwest, the South, and Canada, since the promise of untold riches earned from a few years– trapping seemed vastly preferable to life on a hardscrabble farm.

part" relationships. Movies and novels have planted the idea that these women were called "squaws," but that was a word that amounted to an insult to white men and Native Americans alike. Despite this, men who entered into such relationships were often referred to as "squawmen."

While the mountain men were an eclectic group, and no two were exactly alike, there were some traits that were broadly shared amongst them. It is true that they were all toughened outdoorsmen who ground down the rough edges of the raw wilderness, and it is also true that the majority of them were loners who were fighting a private battle with the rules of a society that they had rejected.

But if they were determined to escape from society, most of them had at least one of its perceived evils branded deep in their souls. By and large, they became mountain men because they believed that there was money in it, and they saw trapping in the Rocky Mountains as a way to get rich quick. Most of them figured that after a few months or, at worst, a year or two, they would be able to take their

Above: The indigenous tribes of the Rockies were willing to trade with the white man in all essentials, including wives. Many of the mountain, men including Jim Beckwourth and Jim Bridger took native brides.

Opposite page: Mountain men wore whatever nature provided. Here, a re-enactor wears an authentic headdress made from a bear's hide and jawbone.

earnings and become big fish in the small pond that was the Pacific Northwest, where destiny had been calling their countrymen.

Many among them, of course, had no intention of going anywhere else; the long arm of the law was waiting back where they came from to make them answer for forgotten crimes of their former life and, to be sure, there were many of those. There were also many who didn't live to see the payoff. During all of the years that they combed the streams and bogs of the Rockies, an average of one mountain man was killed each and every week, and more often than not it was a violent death.

For the most part, though, very few of these men ever joined the hordes of emigrants bound to establish homesteads in the far West. No matter what ideas any of them might have had about trapping as a stepping stone to a better future, they quickly found out that it was their future. Tough as the life may have been, it was an addictive one, and even the men who managed to build substantial bank accounts found it nearly impossible not to stay in the mountains for at least one more stab at gathering up some more of those "hairy dollars," as they called beaver pelts.

Although the fur companies skimmed off the bulk of the profits of their labors and overcharged their trappers for the things they needed at company trading posts, some of the smarter men among them may well have been able to put together a tidy nest egg that could have become their grubstake for an easier life if they didn't gamble it away in the meantime. After all, their money was no good out in the wilderness, and they managed to live reasonably well off the land, so any cash they were able to accumulate was their stake in the future.

And it wasn't as though there wasn't any money floating around out there, even if fur trading never was a major factor in the overall economy back then. During its heyday, about $300,000 worth of furs was shipped from St. Louis every single year. In today's dollars, that comes to more than $3.36 million, and an equal amount flowed in every year in the form of trade goods. Mere peanuts? Possibly; but considering the percentage of the total population that was involved in the beaver trade, it was big business, and it was no wonder that so many young men saw a fast buck in it.

For the most part, these country boys drifted into St. Louis with little more than that vague dream. All they knew for sure was that whatever became of them, they were still far better off than their fathers had been, trying to scratch out a living on hardscrabble farms.

The easiest and most common first step they took was signing on with one of the fur companies as an engagee. They were the lowest of the low in the overall pecking order, expected to do the heavy lifting, trading post and camp housekeeping, and any other chore that the experienced men considered beneath them. Their motivation, obviously, was the hope that one day soon they would be promoted to the status of trapper, with company-supplied traps and animals, and that they might then even be allowed to go off on their own, free to wander wherever they pleased with their own gear and sell their pelts to anyone they cared to. This was the rarest breed of all, and it turned out to be only a dream for the majority of trappers.

For most of these neophytes, it was the first time they had ever done anything and gotten paid for it. An engagee's salary was typically ten or fifteen dollars a month. They were expected to do a bit of trapping in their spare time, but any furs they might bring in became company property, and there were no bonus payments. The company also expected them to pay for all of the things they needed. A new

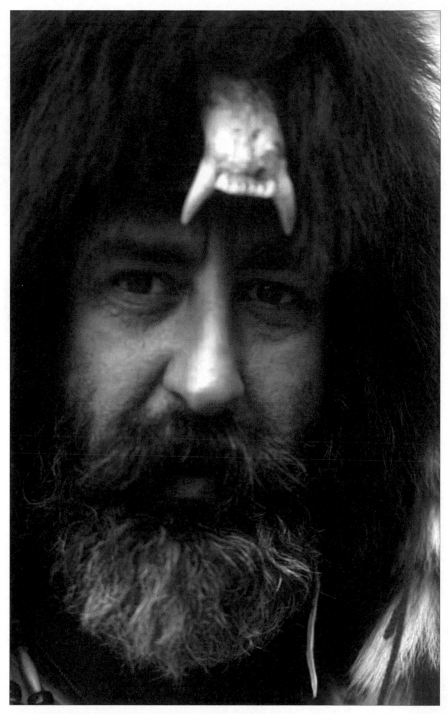

shirt, for instance, could eat up a whole month's pay. Some of them had already done some trapping, usually for muskrat, while they were growing up, but most of them didn't have the slightest idea how to trap and skin a beaver. No matter; they were surrounded by experienced experts, and learning the ropes was easier than learning how to play a guitar.

These apprentices constituted a large part of the entourage when big brigades of trappers went out on their expeditions. Their job was to set up and maintain the night camps and take care of the horses and pack animals. On average, there was one such camp keeper for every three four-footed animals.

Whether they were traveling in brigades of fifty or sixty or in smaller bands of two or three, just about every Rocky Mountain trapper carried the same basic equipment. Along with about six steel beaver traps, each of them toted an Indian blanket, together with a spare pair of wool-lined moccasins to replace the ones they were wearing that would soon wear out. Moccasins might even become a meal of last resort in lean times. They also carried a powder horn and a bullet pouch along with a bullet mold. These items were attached to their belt next to a butcher knife and a whetstone to keep it razor sharp. Each of them also carried flint and steel for making fires, a sheet metal frying pan, and a small wooden box that was filled with heaver bait. Most of these things were carried in what they called their "possibles bag," which they slung over their backs everywhere they went to keep them prepared for just about any possibility. A rawhide pouch around their necks held a pipe and a supply of tobacco that was compressed into long-lasting cakes.

When the tobacco was gone, they would follow the lead of the Indians and smoke what the natives called kinnik-kinnik, the inner bark of the red willow, which they scraped from the trees in thin flakes and dried over a fire before rubbing them into a form that resembled tobacco. But the resemblance ended there. While the nicotine in tobacco leaves produces a soothing

Below: Types of pipe from artifacts found at Rendezvous sites. A pipe was a vital piece of equipment.

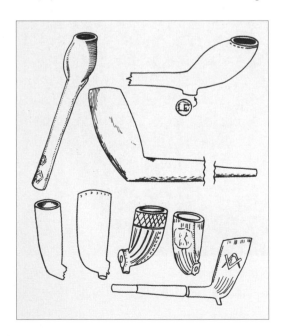

Above: The essentials of a mountain man's life. An authentic collection of equipment:

A. Buffalo hide-covered water canteens

B. Possibles bag in buffalo hide

C. Handmade butcher knife

D. Felt hat with buffalo fur band

E. Pipe

F. Assortment of handmade horn tools

G. Horn spoon

H. Powder horn

I. Buffalo fur gauntlets

effect, kinnik-kinnik has a narcotic effect similar to marijuana. To avoid having to use this substance, most of the trappers packed plenty of tobacco ahead of any expedition. They needed to keep their wits about them out there. If a man's pipe broke, as they often did, he would carve himself a new one with the folding pocket knife that each of them inevitably carried. His pipe was the only companion a mountain man could count on, and many of them considered it the most important part of the paraphernalia they carried.

Most trappers, though certainly not all, also carried a straight razor. Contrary to the popular image of these backwoodsmen, they weren't all bearded. Shaving was the only attempt any of them ever made to look "civilized." There was no hint of anything resembling gentility among these rough and ready adventurers, and it might be expected that they would be a foul-mouthed bunch, like the boatmen whose brawn carried goods on the Mississippi in those pre-steamboat days. But strangely, these men wouldn't as much as say "damn" when things went wrong. The Indians who they emulated didn't have any vulgarities in their languages, either. When they needed to emphasize any strong feelings, Native Americans and mountain men alike had a single all-purpose word, "Waugh!" This was an imitation of the determined growl of a grizzly bear.

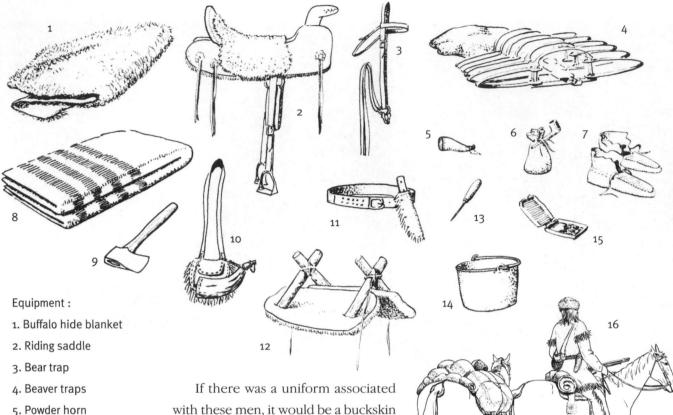

Equipment :

1. Buffalo hide blanket
2. Riding saddle
3. Bear trap
4. Beaver traps
5. Powder horn
6. Tobacco sack and pipe
7. Moccasins
8. Indian blanket
9. Tomahawk
10. Possibles bag
11. Butcher knife in sheath
on belt
12. Pack saddle
13. Awl
14. Iron kettle
15. Flints in striker box
16. The mountain man
with full equipment
mounted on his horse

If there was a uniform associated with these men, it would be a buckskin shirt and sturdy trousers, also made of cured animal skins, usually antelope. They also wore warm moccasins and a wool cap or a wide-brimmed felt hat. Their shirts and leggings were fringed in the manner that was made popular by Buffalo Bill's Wild West Show in the next generation, but the fringe wasn't entirely a decorative touch. The rawhide strips, which they called "whangs," could be cut off and used to repair snags in their clothes. Such damage was common among these men who spent so much time crawling through thick underbrush. They also decorated their outfits with porcupine quills that came in handy as needles, although each man also carried an awl for tougher repair jobs. After a few weeks of roaming the mountains, their clothes, and even their hats, became stained with grease and blood from skinning beaver and butchering game. Combined with the smoke from their campfires, it quickly gave the shiny look of leather to their outfits.

Most mountain men carried steel tomahawks—as hatchets were called in this Indian country—on their saddles. They usually had a rifle for hunting game as well

Left: The buckskin shirt and leggings which were standard mountain men apparel. These were fringed, which was not merely a decorative touch; the rawhide strips were called "whangs" and could be cut off in emergency to repair clothes torn by crawling through the thorny underbrush in search of game or avoiding hostile tribes.

Far left: Warm fur-lined moccasins were also standard mountain man garb. They were easier to repair or replace than store-bought boots and better for silent tracking. In extreme cases of hardship they could be boiled to provide a survival meal. These were often traded from local Indian tribes.

as a pistol for protection against rattlesnakes and nasty varmints. This could also be used as the weapon of last resort in an Indian fight. At first, the majority of them carried the M. 1803 rifle that was standard military issue in the early nineteenth century and had been used by Lewis and Clark's men. But over time the gun was modified to become the shorter plains rifle that suited them best. These weapons could drop a thousand-pound buffalo and even a grizzly bear, not to mention an attacking Indian brave, with a single well-placed shot.

The bulk of the plains rifles were made by gunsmiths Jacob Hawken and his brother Samuel of St. Louis, Missouri. They ran their St. Louis shop between 1815 and 1858. These forty-inch guns, whose range was about two-hundred yards, fired a half-ounce lead ball with a modified flintlock mechanism, and each weighed about twelve pounds. Percussion rifles began appearing around this time, but the trappers generally stuck to the flintlocks that they were used to. Plus, since these weapons didn't need a supply of caps to ignite the charge, mountain men regarded them as more convenient.

The inside of the plains rifle barrel was scored with grooves that gave a spin to the bullet and made its course true all the way to the limits of the weapon's range. But the mountain men were all crack shots anyway. Most of them were

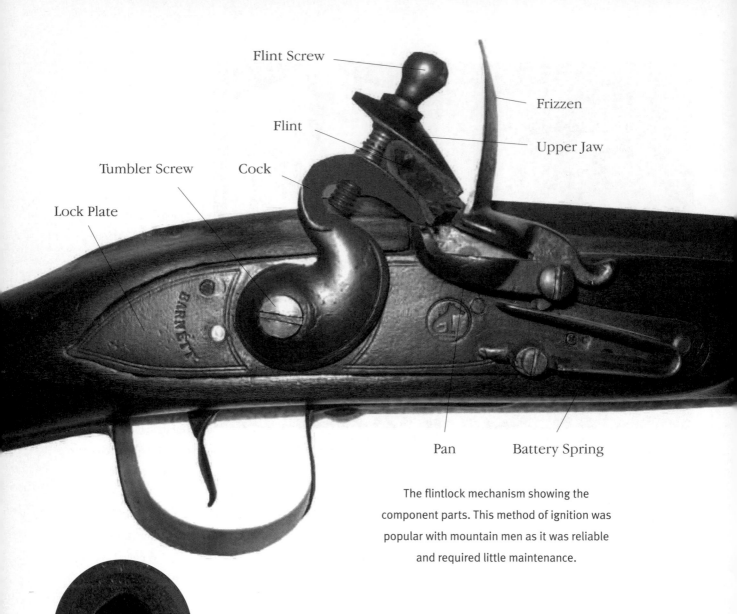

Flint Screw

Frizzen

Flint

Upper Jaw

Tumbler Screw

Cock

Lock Plate

BARNETT

Pan

Battery Spring

The flintlock mechanism showing the
component parts. This method of ignition was
popular with mountain men as it was reliable
and required little maintenance.

Above: The muzzle of a .50
caliber rifled Plains Rifle,
which plainly shows the ri-
fling grooves on the inside
of the barrel.

in the prime of life, their hands steady and their eyes sharp, and the majority
had been handling rifles from the time they were first able to stand. Typically,
they could hit a two-inch blaze on a tree a hundred yards away, and then put
another ball right on top of it. They were forever competing with one another,
whenever time became heavy on their hands, with such demonstrations of
marksmanship as snuffing out a candle with a bullet fired from fifty feet away
and even cutting bullets in two by shooting the edge of a sharp axe from the
same distance.

The mountain men sometimes carried their gunpowder in lead boxes that could
also be melted down to make their bullets. This innovation had been developed by

Meriwether Lewis when he outfitted his own expedition. Their bullets were interchangeable between their rifles and their pistols.

Their deadly skill with a rifle was not lost on the Indians, many of whom had been armed by the British trappers as well as the American companies. The intent was for the Indians to use the rifles as a replacement for their traditional arrows and spears when hunting for food and buffalo skins. But, of course, they also used them to defend their territory against the trappers. In some instances they were able to take the superior Hawken rifles in battle, but for the most part they were armed with inferior weapons known as "Indian Trade rifles" that were less powerful and much less accurate. The mountain men also had an advantage because Native Americans tended not to be fastidious about keeping their guns clean and in good repair, which amounted to a fetish among the white trappers.

The most productive time for beaver trapping was in the fall, between the middle of October and the first two weeks of November. This was when the streams began to freeze over. The beaver had acquired their winter coats by then, and the fur was at its silky finest. There was another flurry of activity around April when the ice broke up, and the animals became active once more, still wearing their winter coats. In the months between, the trappers hibernated together in winter camps, although if the take had been slim in the fall, they sometimes did chop through the ice to get at their quarry and surprise them curled up in their dens in the midst of their long winter naps. Winter was also a time for the more intrepid mountain men to scout new territory, but most of all it was a time to swap stories, do some reading, or to play cards and dice. Most trappers were literate; a few were even college graduates.

One of the earliest published eyewitness descriptions of these winter camps might well have served as a recruiting brochure for the fur companies: "Nothing can be more social and cheering than the welcome blaze of a campfire on a cold winter's night," it said, "and nothing more amusing or entertaining, if not instructive, than the rough conversations of the single-minded mountaineers. Their simple daily talk is all of exciting adventure, since their whole existence is spent in scenes of peril and privation. Consequently, the narration of their daily life is a tale of thrilling accidents and hairbreadth escapes which, though matter-of-fact to them, appear a startling romance to those who are not acquainted with the lives led by these men. With the sky for a roof and their rifles to supply them with food and clothing, they call no man lord or master, and are as free as the game they follow."

Below: A fancy copper powder flask with a stamped and patterned body. This factory-made type gradually replaced the earlier leather and horn versions of the flask.

Plains Rifles

The first mountain men used military rifles, many of which had hardly evolved from the War of Independence. A particular favorite was the 1803 Model U.S. flintlock rifle, Harpers Ferry Model. Also modified versions of the French Charleville muskets which were imported at the time of the war with Britain. Although the percussion system appeared later in the period many mountain men stayed with the flintlock system because it was reliable and didn't require a supply of caps at a time when every item had to be carried into the mountains.

Above: Harpers Ferry Model 1803 U.S.
Another example of the 1803 rifle but with
a modified barrel of 32 inches.

Above: Specifications –
Caliber: .41 inch Barrel: 40 inches, octagonal
Stock: maple with brass fore-end cap.

The Model 1830's lock bears the mark, "Harpers Ferry 1819."

Above: Harpers Ferry Model 1803 U.S. Flintlock rifle with detail of lock.
Specifications – Caliber: .54 inch Barrel: 36 inches, part octagonal Brass Fittings: ramrod
pipes, buttplate, patchbox, and trigger guard Stock: walnut.

Below: Kentucky Flintlock Rifle The backwoodsmen used the longer, heavier,
but smaller-bore Kentucky rifles and many of these found their way up into the mountains.
Ultimately, though, they lacked the stopping power needed for larger game.

Below: Unmarked Full Stock Flintlock Kentucky Rifle with engravings on patchbox.
Specifications – Caliber: 32 inch Barrel: 36 inch, octagonal Stock: maple.

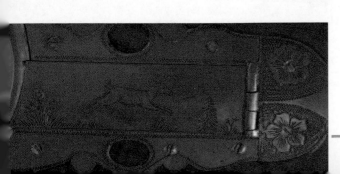

Left: Close up of the intricate engraving which
characterized many of the mountain men's guns.
This scene depicts a deer fleeing a hunter, with
floral motifs.

Hawken Plains Rifles

To satisfy the demand for accurate rifles a number of gunsmiths set up shop in St Louis 'The Gateway to the West' which was the jumping off point for all expeditions up river into the mountains. Jacob Hawken and his brother Samuel were two such men. Their name became synonymous with the 'Plains Rifles' that they manufactured.

Essentially the Plains Rifle was required to have a heavy but relatively short octagonal barrel. Calibers were large- usually over .45 inch for good stopping power for large game like Buffalo or Grizzly Bears. No good hitting either with a .36! That would just make 'em mad. The guns were half stocked and were required to have a high

Below: Heavy S. Hawken St. Louis Plains Rifle.

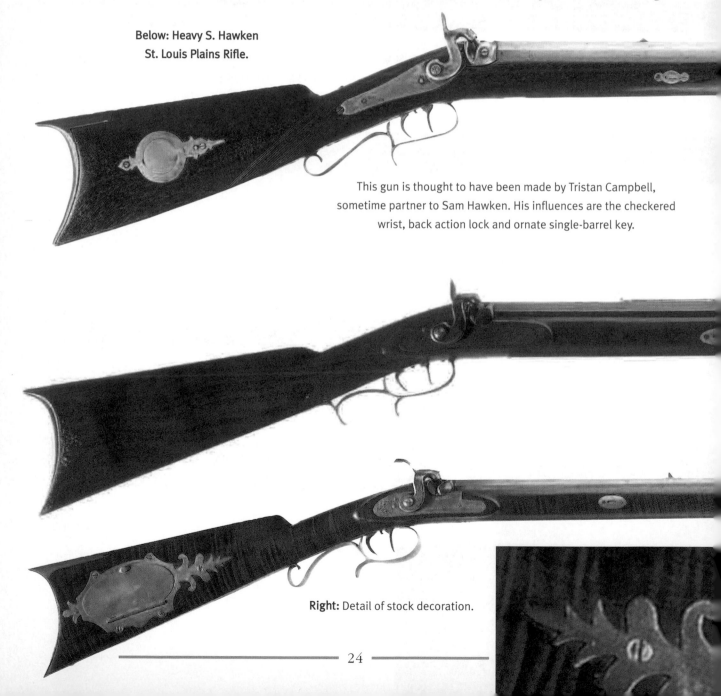

This gun is thought to have been made by Tristan Campbell, sometime partner to Sam Hawken. His influences are the checkered wrist, back action lock and ornate single-barrel key.

Right: Detail of stock decoration.

standard of finish, ornate patch boxes, scrolled trigger guards ,fancy hammers and engraved lock plates. A gun was probably, apart from his pipe, a mountain man's most treasured possession and he was prepared to spend a bit extra to get a good one.

Above: Samuel Hawken's mark on the barrel of St. Louis Plains Rifle.

Specifications –
Caliber: .45 inch
Barrel: octagonal
Stock: walnut.

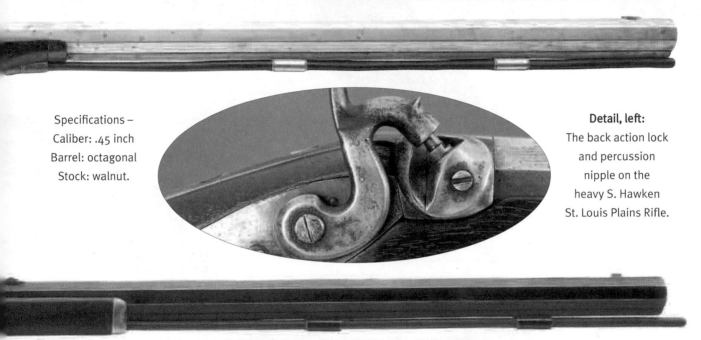

Detail, left:
The back action lock and percussion nipple on the heavy S. Hawken St. Louis Plains Rifle.

Above: Hawken Shop Gemmer Percussions Half Stock Rifle
In 1864 J. P. Gemmer bought out the Hawken business and continued to make guns in the
Hawken tradition until 1915. This example is a late plains rifle but retains all of the classic characteristics.
Guns of this type continued to be used on the frontier for many years.

Above: A Classic Two Pin Half-Stock Percussion Rifle
This gun is marked "S. Hawken St. Louis" on the top of the barrel
and is a fine example of a longer-barreled, fancier-wooded
(high grade tiger stripe maple in this case) plains rifle.

Handguns

As with Rifles the main source of handguns available to the mountain man would have been military issue weapons. Expensive fancy European imports were probably outside of the average trappers budget so he would rely on the US martial models of the day. These too would be Flintlock and we have already seen that he preferred this mechanism for practical reasons. The pistol would have been carried for personal protection rather than for hunting as it is quicker to swing into action than a heavy plains rifle. It could be worn on the belt and be taken places that a rifle couldn't so in a way this was a prelude to the Gunslingers of the Frontier.

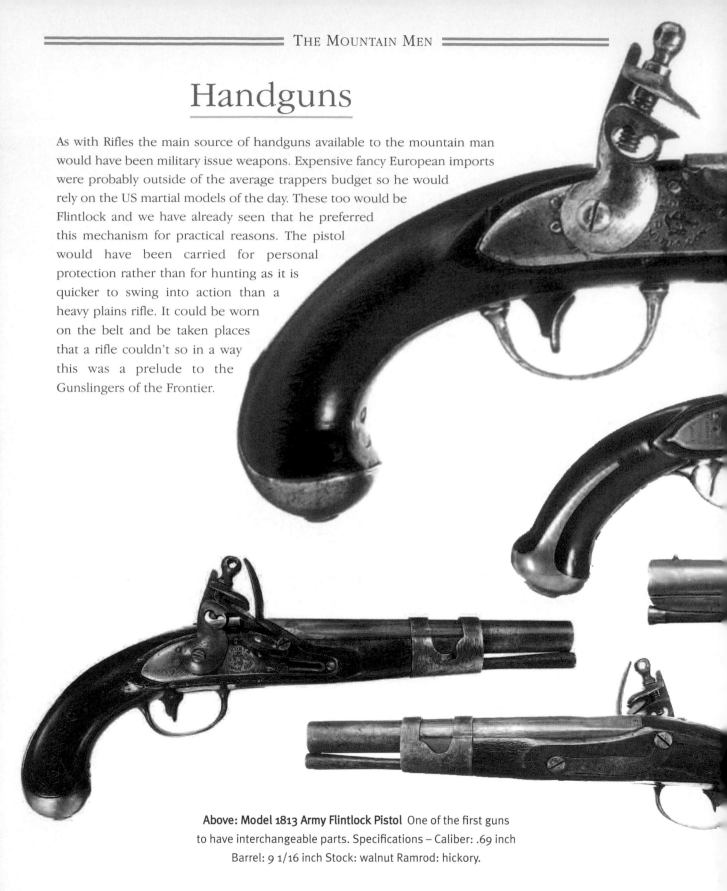

Above: Model 1813 Army Flintlock Pistol One of the first guns to have interchangeable parts. Specifications – Caliber: .69 inch Barrel: 9 1/16 inch Stock: walnut Ramrod: hickory.

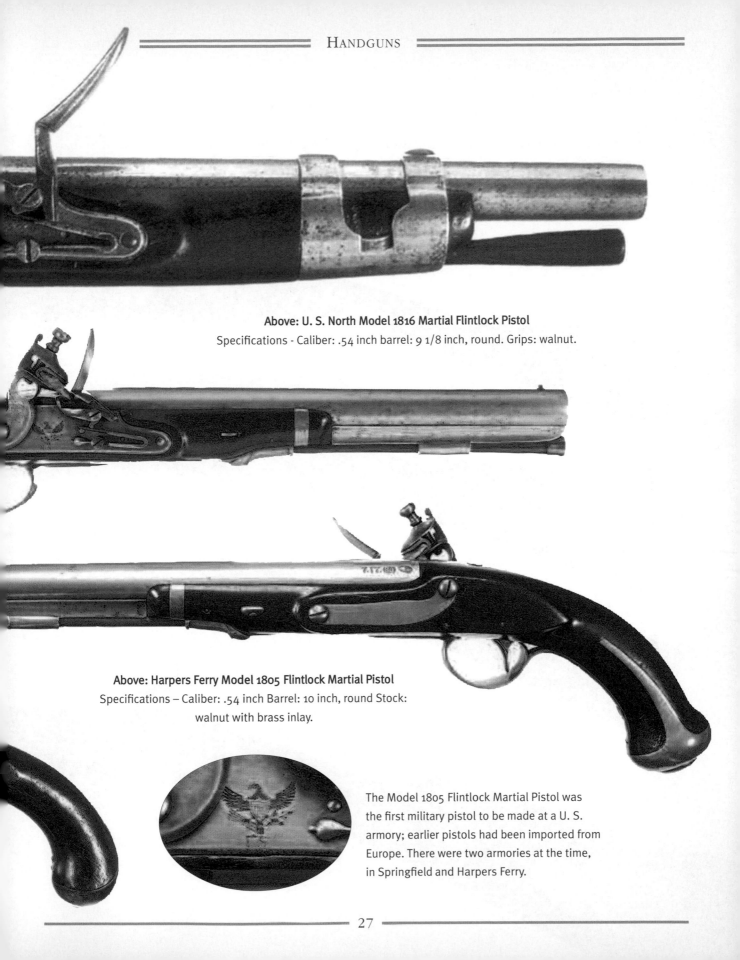

Above: U. S. North Model 1816 Martial Flintlock Pistol
Specifications - Caliber: .54 inch barrel: 9 1/8 inch, round. Grips: walnut.

Above: Harpers Ferry Model 1805 Flintlock Martial Pistol
Specifications – Caliber: .54 inch Barrel: 10 inch, round Stock:
walnut with brass inlay.

The Model 1805 Flintlock Martial Pistol was
the first military pistol to be made at a U. S.
armory; earlier pistols had been imported from
Europe. There were two armories at the time,
in Springfield and Harpers Ferry.

Trade Muskets

These guns were the main weapon of the Indians in the time of the mountain men and were basically guns that had been traded to them by outfits like the Hudson's Bay Company in return for precious furs. They were for the most part inferior guns to those at the disposal of the mountain men and to those of the British Army just over the border in Canada. This was obviously

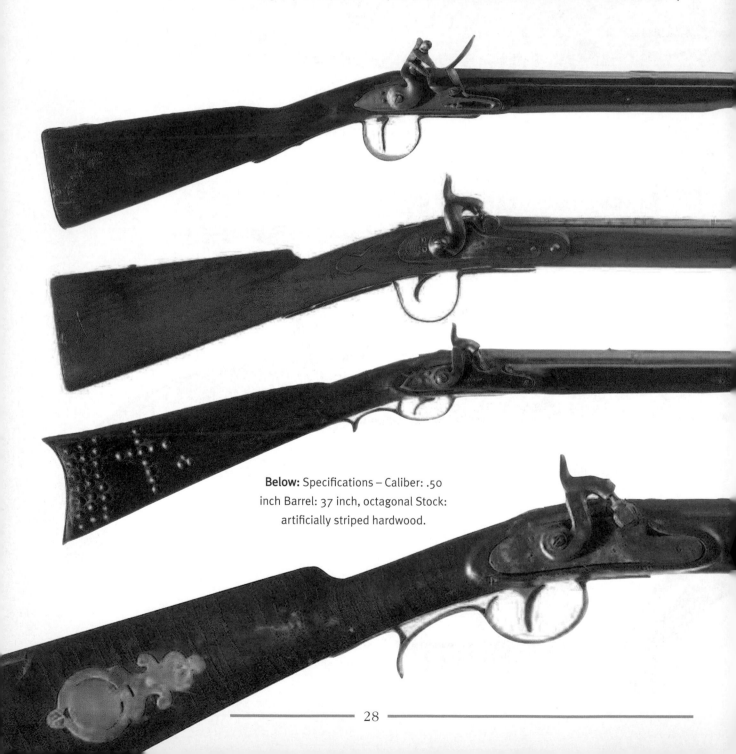

Below: Specifications – Caliber: .50 inch Barrel: 37 inch, octagonal Stock: artificially striped hardwood.

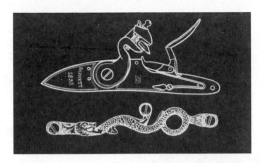

Left: Flintlock mechanism of Barnett Trade Rifle.

part of the plan. They were designed to be simple but robust as it was believed that the indians did not have the aptitude for maintenance and care that the white man did. Despite this several excellently kept examples have survived.

Above: Barnett London Indian Trade Flint Musket
Specifications – Caliber: .62 inch, smoothbore Barrel: 40 inches, octagonal breech/round barrel
Stock: walnut, marked Barnett London.

Above: Hudson's Bay Indian Trade Musket by Hollis & Sons, Makers to Her Majesty.
Specifications – Caliber: .58 inch Barrel: 36 inches, round Stock: hardwood.

Above: Early Ketland Northwest Indian Trade Musket
A good example of Indian brass tack decoration on the stock, which is dark tiger maple. The gun has been converted from flintlock to percussion cap. Specifications – Caliber: .60 inch Barrel: 35 inches, octagonal/round smoothbore.

Above: H.E. Leman Indian Trade Rifle, marked H.E. Leman Lancaster Pa.
This gun is something of a step forward, in that it is of a superior design from a U.S. gunsmith, and is actually rifled. A similar gun was captured from the Sioux after the Custer battle, so it was still considered a useful weapon in 1876.

Right: Surviving the winter called for plenty of fuel. A sharp saw and a strong elbow were two essential tools for any mountain man.

In fact, trapping beaver was a matter more of experience than special skill. Although these nocturnal animals are almost never actually seen in the wild, the dams they build out of logs, sticks, twigs, and mud across streams often are as much as a hundred feet long, and the lodges behind them are simple to spot. But sometimes those sites may have been abandoned, and the only way to know for sure was to look for signs of recent maintenance, which took a practiced eye. The trappers knew that the surest beaver sign was trees with freshly gnawed bark near willow-bordered streams and creeks. Many more of these rodents lived in burrows under riverbanks and in marshy areas abounding in cottonwood, and it took an even keener eye to figure out where they might be. But that was only the first step.

Next, the trapper had to locate the entrance to their dens, moving stealthily so that the creatures wouldn't know he was there. Then he needed to find a spot in the shallow water near the burrow's entrance, where a beaver was most likely to emerge. After that, he readied his steel trap before he placed it there, and that was no easy trick, either. The powerful springs had to be depressed while he set the jaws into the open position, ready to grab its prey. If a man wasn't careful, they

Below: "Nothing can be more social and cheering than the welcome blaze of a campfire on a cold winters night" – *early published eyewitness to trappers camp.*

Beaver Traps

Inset: A beaver swims across a quarry's lake. Below: A beaver lodge in the kind of unspoiled setting that the mountain men would have encountered.

There were many traps available to the mountain men. In the early years of the nineteenth century there was no way to mass-produce traps and they were all made by hand by a blacksmith. The best types used double springs to close the jaws. A chain attached the trap to the bottom of the stream which effectively caused the beaver to drown when caught in the jaws. This meant that setting the traps was a particularly dangerous and uncomfortable occupation.

Larger versions of the traps were used to trap wolves and bear but all used the same basic technology. The example shown below was manufactured by the S. Newhouse Community of Oneida , Lititz , Pennsylvania. They also made traps in Sherrill, New York and Niagara Falls, Canada. The traps were numbered according to the type of animal they were designed for–number 4 for Beaver up to 14 for wolf and mountain lion, 15 for bear. The name of the company is cast around the rim of the circular pan.

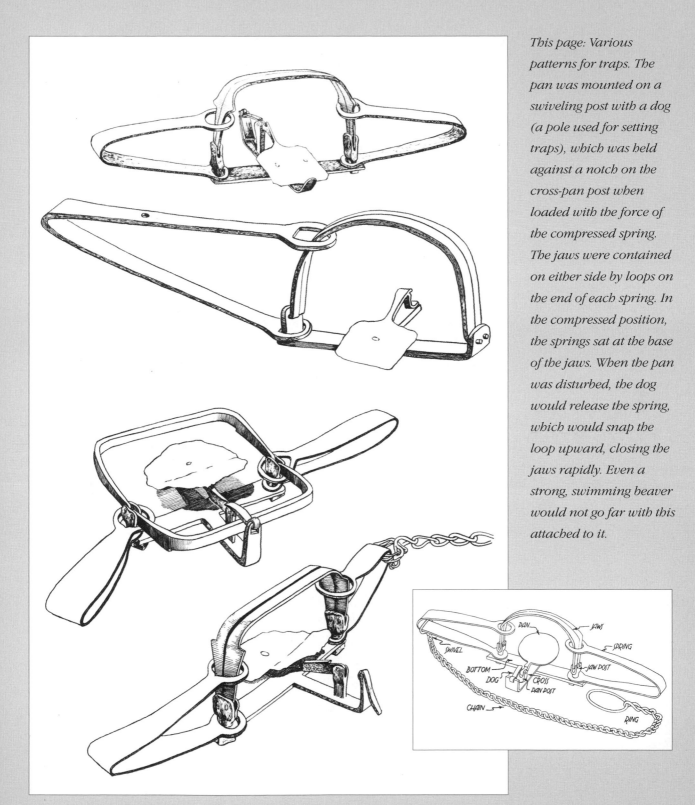

This page: Various patterns for traps. The pan was mounted on a swiveling post with a dog (a pole used for setting traps), which was held against a notch on the cross-pan post when loaded with the force of the compressed spring. The jaws were contained on either side by loops on the end of each spring. In the compressed position, the springs sat at the base of the jaws. When the pan was disturbed, the dog would release the spring, which would snap the loop upward, closing the jaws rapidly. Even a strong, swimming beaver would not go far with this attached to it.

could spring back and break his hand. The trap had a chain attached to it, which the trapper fastened to a pole that he drove into the stream bottom. Before wading into the icy water to put the trap in place, he daubed a bit of beaver bait onto the pole, placed a fresh willow branch on the trap's pan, and then quietly went on his way to set another trap in the same way. He then splashed water onto his tracks to cover his scent. On an average day, a man could set as many as six traps in this way.

The beaver bait, or "medicine," as both the trappers and the Native American hunters called it, was a homemade concoction with a base of oil that was extracted from glands under the beaver's tail. Known as castoreum, this is the substance that the animal uses to mark the limits of its territory. Most mountain men mixed it with ground spices like nutmeg and cinnamon to add to its potency, following a time-honored recipe originally developed by the Indians. This embellishment probably wasn't necessary. Especially during the early winter mating season, the castoreum was generally powerful enough all by itself to make any beaver sit up on its hind legs and take notice. And that was exactly the point; the beaver's hind paws are quite a bit larger than those in front, so they were the trap's target. Once it was caught in the powerful steel jaws, the panicked animal would inevitably swim for deeper water, where the five-pound trap dragged it to the bottom and held it there until it drowned.

The dawn hours were spent retrieving the victims, then skinning them and preparing the pelts. The meat is edible, but unless the larder was low, it was usually cast aside and wound up as dinner for some hungry wolf. The broad flat tail, on the other hand, was, they

Below: Patterns of axe and tomahawk heads used by the mountain men.

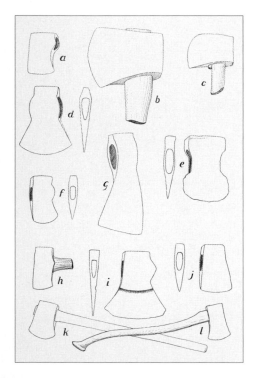

Left: Trapping beaver was only possible in the winter by breaking the ice around their lodges. Their coats were especially lustrous during the winter months and therefore more valuable.

say, a tasty meal roasted over a campfire, and it was almost always saved.

Mountain men could hardly have been called gourmets. As far as they were concerned, "meat's meat," and nothing that ran, slithered, or flew was considered unfit to eat. Although they routinely waded through the best trout streams on the North American continent, and trapped along rivers teeming with salmon, they didn't have the time or the patience for fishing. When they could get it, buffalo was a terrific source of food, mostly because there was so much of it from a single kill. Buffalo livers and tongues, usually eaten raw while they were still warm from a recently killed animal, were a kind of delicacy to them. They also looked forward to meals of venison, mutton (from big horn sheep), mountain goats, turkey, grouse, and other wildfowl. Like the Indians, they considered dog meat an especially tasty treat, and when they had a choice, it was usually their number-two favorite for its

Above: Making the set.

richness and flavor. But number one on everybody's list was the meat of the cougar, which always made a memorable meal, even if these mountain lions were hard to kill. The mountain men also sometimes ate their horses and mules when there was nothing else to be found, but the meat of the beaver ranked several notches below rattlesnake, and they rarely saved it.

They did, of course, always save the castoreum— not only to make more beaver bait, but to sell to perfume makers, who treasured the musk almost as much as hat makers lusted after the beavers' fur. The pelts themselves were stretched on willow hoops and set out for drying in the sun before being marked with the company brand and compressed into packs ready for market.

Left: Types of fall traps used for larger game such as elk. Though this was not the mountain man's main quarry, he had to stock his larder.

Above: Types of beaver trap.

Left: Trappers setting fire to the prairie in order to get the buffalo herd to stampede.

Above: Indians stampeding buffalo into a box canyon to achieve a kill.

Above: Slaughtered buffalo ready for butchering.

Above: Two authentically-dressed re-enactors prepare their plains rifles for action.

Right: In later life, Thomas Fiztpatrick became one of the more successful ex-mountain men. Like many of his contemporaries, he became a prominent pillar of his community.

Each individual pelt, which usually weighed about a pound-and-a-half, measured anywhere from eighteen inches to three feet in diameter after drying. Dry pelts were then folded, fur side in, into bundles of sixty. Along with their outer wrapping of deerskin, the bundles weighed about a hundred pounds and had a market value of around $600. The bands of trappers were constantly on the move, and it wasn't practical for them to lug those heavy bales of furs along with them. Instead, they concealed them along the way, together with the supplies and equipment they would need on their eventual journey out of the hunting grounds. These so-called caches were six- or seven-foot pits. These were usually dug as a small hole on high ground and hollowed out much wider at the bottom than at the top, in the

Left: The meat and hide of the buffalo were greatly valued both as a means of survival and as tradable commodities.

general shape of a bell. They were carefully lined with sticks and leaves to avoid damage from dampness. After depositing their stash, like pirates burying treasure, the trappers filled the hole with dirt and then carefully restored the area around it. This was so that their competitors or curious animals wouldn't be likely to find it. The job of camouflaging a cache site was an art in itself, because it also had to be made invisible to the practiced eyes of Native Americans, who were sensitive to every broken twig and even the most subtle changes in the ground under their feet.

But of all the threats to their concealed goods, it was other trapping parties that were most likely to run off with them. Tom Fitzpatrick, one of the most successful of the mountain men, once reported the loss of fifty-five packs of skins all marked with the R.M.F brand used by the Rocky Mountain Fur Company. They eventually

Below: Stalking buffalo required patience. The animals were wary and easily spooked. A powerful rifle was necessaryto give the hunter a greater chance of a kill at long distance.

turned up in a Crow village, where the Indian residents claimed that the skins belonged to the rival American Fur Company and had been left with them for safekeeping. The competitors finally admitted that they had stolen Fitzpatrick's cache and paid for the furs, but such thefts rarely ended so smoothly.

The biggest expense involved in this business, apart from the pittance the companies paid the trappers, was the cost of the traps themselves. The price varied, but eight dollars apiece seems to have been the average. Styles varied, too, but by that time, the preferred one for beaver was a double-springed steel model that had evolved over many years. These traps are still the standard in use today where beaver is hunted. Modern beaver trappers are often farmers and their young sons, who sell furs to companies like Stetson. Stetson's finest felt cowboy hats are still made of beaver fur.

There was no way to mass-produce traps in the early nineteenth century; every single one had to be made by hand by a blacksmith. They hammered them out with amazing speed, but the price they had to charge to make a living themselves made these devices dearly prized by the trappers.

Above and both on opposite page: Beaver pelts were stretched on a willow hoop and hung up to dry. The pelts were then compressed into bundles using a crude wood press. The bundles were then wrapped in hide, ready for transportation.

Right: Jedediah Smith's blacksmith making a bear trap. Most traps used at this time were made by a blacksmith.

The Secret Cache

Opposite page top, and below: Atmospheric depictions of cache pits being loaded and concealed, secretly and at night. Precautions were taken to avoid revealing the location of the cache to keep its valuable contents from being stolen.

Mountain men often spent anything up to two years in the wilderness amassing pelts. Because they were limited by how many they could physically carry with them they evolved the technique of concealing caches of pelts underground in a pit which they could collect on their way back to the trading post or fort. These secret hoards needed to be well camouflaged to avoid being dug up by wolves, rival trappers or Indians. There was skill required in concealing the entrance to look like the earth had not been disturbed – disguising any tell-tale signs that could alert the cache robber. In some cases caches have been found still sealed up 170 years later, which would either indicate that the trapper's concealment was so expert that he could not find the hoard or that he had met a gruesome fate and that the secret of the cache's location went with him to the grave.

*Lower left: Gros Ventre
Indians robbing a
cache. They could trade
these pelts for guns and
other commodities.*

Big Doin's

Below: Map showing the Rendezvous sites from 1825 to 1840, the peak years of the mountain men.

The years between 1825 and 1840 were the heyday of the mountain man. During these years, late summer in the Rockies was a time for a little lying and bragging, re-establishing old friendships and making new ones. The mountain men also got paid for their year's work, and spent their money on supplies for another year of facing down danger posed by Indian natives, rampaging grizzly bears, sudden avalanches, and snowdrifts deep enough to swallow a horse. Most of all, it was an excuse to forget about those things, to cut loose and have a grand old time.

This annual outdoor gathering was known as the "Rocky Mountain Rendezvous." It was the cornerstone of a whole new way of doing business that changed all of the rules that had been followed in the North American fur trade over almost three-hundred years, an innovation that eased the expansion of the United States into

Three Forks

Yellowstone River

Oregon Country

Pierre's Hole
1832

Grand Teton

Bighorn

Fort Hall

Snake River

Riverton 1830
1838

Lander
1829

Fort Laramie

Horse Creek
1833

Cove
1826
1831

Sweet
Lake
1827
1828

1835
1836
1837
1838
1840

South Pass

Hams Fork
1834

N Platte River

Burnt Fork
1825

Green River

Oregon and California and gave birth to this amazing breed that was called the mountain men.

The Rendezvous brought hundreds of independent trappers out from the depths of the mountains. Whole Indian villages would relocate for the occasion in order to get first crack at the new trade goods that were hauled out from St. Louis by men whose profits on them were almost never less than a thousand

Right: Mules were useful for transporting heavy provisions like this barrel of rum, en route to a trapper's Rendezvous.

percent. The fairs lasted anywhere from a couple of days to several weeks, depending on how long it took for everyone's money and credit to run out.

It was always a wild party, and getting drunk was a big part of it. The Monongahela whiskey from Pittsburgh or Jamaican Rum was watered down and the price jacked up, but it did the job, and any man who could remember what he said and what he did last night just wasn't trying hard enough. Those who could remember generally recalled a night of wildly dancing what they called the fandango. In reality, the dance involved improvised shaking and high stepping that was more like Indian ceremonial dances than the real fandango, a fancy triple-time Spanish-inspired dance style that was all the rage down below the Red River in those days.

Above: Sweet Lake, which was the site for the 1827 and 1828 Rendezvous.

1825 ROCKY MOUNTAIN RENDEZVOUS

"When all had come in, he (Ashley) opened his goods, and there was a general jubilee.... We constituted quite a little town, numbering at least eight hundred souls, ...half were women and children. There were some...who had not seen any groceries, such as coffee, sugar, etc. for several months. The whiskey went off as freely as water, even at the exorbitant price he sold it for. All kinds of sports were indulged in with a heartiness that would astonish more civilized societies."

Taken from, *The Life and Adventures of James P. Beckwourth*, as told to Thomas D. Bonner, this passage describes a raucus social event: the rendezvous. Here, mountain men swapped stories, tested their skills, and shared news of friends. The annual event was actually begun as a time saving measure whereby trappers could replenish supplies and trade furs, without traveling to St. Louis each summer. North of this point on Henrys Fork of the Green River, between Birch and Burnt Fork Creeks, the first Rocky Mountain Rendezvous was held during June and July, 1825. Held under the direction of William Ashley the gathering was planned for the Green River, but was moved up Henrys Fork because that site provided better forage for animals. One-hundred twenty trappers gathered to barter their furs at Burnt Fork. Among those assembled were some of the industry's most colorful characters; General Ashley, Jedediah Smith, Bill Sublette, Davey Jackson, Tom Fitzpatrick, Etienne Provost, James Beckwourth and a still green Jim Bridger. On July 2, 1825, Ashley and his men headed for St. Louis with a load of furs worth $50,000.

Held annually throughout the region until 1840, when the demand for beaver pelts decreased, the rendezvous is remembered as one of the western frontiers most colorful traditions. Modern day mountain men still reenact these 19th century "fur fairs".

Above: Plaque commemorating the very first Rendezvous at Burnt Fork on the Green River.

Right: Wild dancing, drinking, and smoking were the order of the day at the annual Rendezvous.

These men who came together every summer were all gamblers by nature, but they didn't often cast dice or deal out poker hands. Theirs was a much simpler game that involved holding out a pair of fists with a pebble hidden in one of them, and challenging anyone willing to take a chance to guess which hand contained the pebble. The odds were good and cheating appeared to be impossible, so the stakes were usually high. Stories of men losing their horses or guns or— especially in the case of Native Americans, who also loved the game— even their wives, were quite common. There was at least one tale of a man who bet his scalp on a pick of the hands and lost. It is fairly likely that he didn't pay off the debt willingly, though. Many didn't, and bloody brawls brought on by welshers were as much a part of these summer get-togethers as impromptu horse races, wrestling matches, and tomahawk throwing competitions.

Above: In the Rocky Mountains of western Wyoming, a mountain meadow pond reflects the gathered tepees of a Rendezvous gathering.

Right: Horses ride into a recreated Rendezvous.

Below: The mountain men adopted the survival skills of the Native Americans to cope with the same harsh environment. Like the natives, they constructed tepees for shelter.

When all else failed, disputes between mountain men were settled with duels, but not the usual "pistols at twenty paces" sort of thing. These men faced each other with long rifles, and every one of them was a well-practiced dead shot.

Beaver trappers roamed the Rocky Mountains for about thirty years, but mountain men dominated the trade for only about half that long. The country hasn't ever seen the likes of them before or since, and although calling them civilized would have been fighting words to these men, they had a greater impact on our idea of American civilization as an example of unfettered freedom and self-reliance than whole generations of soldiers, preachers, and politicians.

Furs, Fashions, and Fabulous Fortunes

At the heart of it all was the demand for beaver skins, which began to have an impact on American history when French trappers started harvesting them, long before the English established themselves along the Eastern Seaboard. It was all in the service of fashion; more specifically, the making of men's hats. No European or American dandy could possibly consider himself well-dressed without at least one beaver hat. Whole armies were outfitted with them, and even George Washington's trademark tricorner hat was made of beaver fur. Farmers wore them when they decked themselves out in their Sunday best, and no lawyer or doctor could expect to be taken seriously if he wasn't wearing a high-crowned beaver hat. Even some of the mountain men themselves wore broad-brimmed versions, but — unlike just about everything else they wore — they didn't make them themselves.

That was a job for professional hatters, and there were thousands of them doing a thriving business both in Europe and in the United States. The beaver pelt that was the basis of their craft is an oily skin that is covered with coarse hair layered over fine fur, known as wool. The hatter would shave off the two layers of fur and

Above: Hide scale for measuring the weight of beaver pelts.

Above: John Jacob Astor, the founder of the American Fur Company, who became the richest man in America.

Left: Pelts being loaded up at the trading post or fort to be shipped back east by river to the hat factories.

Right: Beautiful but remote places like this beaver lodge in Jackson Hole, Wyoming, were invaded to provide hats for people back East.

Below: The craze for beaver hats lasted about fifty years, from the latter part of the eighteenth century to the 1840s. George Washington's tricorner hat was made from beaver fur. A surprising number of other popular styles, including the cowboy stetson, were made in the same way.

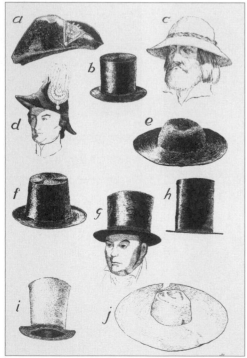

separate them before selling the remaining skin to glue factories. The wool was then placed on a mold and manipulated into shape under sprays of hot water, while bits of the coarser fur were gradually mixed in to add strength in a process called felting.

When the matted mass was beginning to resemble a hat, shellac was daubed on the underside to give it more strength, and fine fur was applied to the outside to give it a velvety look. The demand for the hats continued over many generations, long enough to make the beaver extinct in Europe and almost non-existent in Eastern North America as well. Silk hats helped to cover the shortage, as did less luxurious fur hats made from the pelt of the nutria, the beaver's close cousin, which abounded in South America. But there was still an almost desperate demand for the higher-quality, water-resistant beaver fur; when the Lewis and Clark expedition crossed the Rockies in 1804, they described a country teeming with beaver. Suddenly, it seemed as though the drought might have ended.

John Jacob Astor, who had become the richest man in America trading for furs in New York's Adirondack Mountains, established a base at the mouth of the Columbia River in 1810, and sent a supply ship out from New York that he planned to use to ship furs across the Pacific and build a new market in China. At the same time, he sent a party overland from St. Louis to scout sites for inland trading posts that would unite the operations of his American Fur Company's Northwest base with fur-rich territory north of the Missouri River.

Although this was an attempt to get in on the ground floor in the West, Astor's men weren't alone out there. Russian fur traders had already established themselves along the Alaska coast, and the British considered the whole Northwest their private turf. Their Hudson's Bay Company ranged through the Canadian

Below: A beaver (inset) and a beaver dam – seen here at South Piney, Wyoming – were the bread and butter of mountain men, who trapped the animal for its fur.

Right: Indians were suspicious of the early American explorers, and clashes often resulted in deaths on both sides.

Above: Fort Astoria was established at the mouth of the Columbia River in 1810 in what is now Oregon.

forests all the way from the Atlantic to the Pacific, and they were ready to do anything it might take to eliminate any competition. They frequently paid the Indians who gathered the furs more than the going price for pelts as a way of cornering the market, even though it meant taking a loss. But they were prepared to be far more ruthless than that.

After Lewis and Clark crossed the mountains six years earlier, the English saw the writing on the wall and dispatched brigades down across the Canadian border intent on creating what they characterized as a "beaver desert" before the American trappers could get their act together. They also used their considerable experience with the Indians to stoke the Blackfoot Indians' suspicion of Americans. This distrust had begun when two Blackfoot braves were killed by Lewis and Clark's men, and was exacerbated by the trading partnership early American trappers had established with the Crow, who were ancient enemies of the Blackfoot.

Some time later, a truce was negotiated between the Americans and the Piegan branch of the Blackfoot nation, who dominated the central Rockies. Only traders would be allowed into Piegan territory; trappers still risked almost certain death if they crossed the line. But this area was also the very heart of beaver country, and fighting Blackfeet was a grim fact of life for every mountain man willing to venture into Blackfoot land.

Above: A Blackfoot tepee. The creators of these highly decorative structures were the sworn enemies of the mountain men.

The War of 1812 between Britain and the United States changed everything on the Pacific Coast, and the ripples were felt back in the Rockies. Astor was forced to sell his burgeoning empire to his English competitors, who expanded their holdings to the south and east under what they called the North West Company, effectively leaving the Americans out in the cold. But the Louisiana Purchase had made much of the region a part of the United States, and Congress eventually passed a law declaring that Indian trade along the upper Missouri River was off-limits to anyone but American citizens. The government backed up the statute by moving a token number of cavalry troops into the area. That encouraged Astor to re-establish his American Fur Company in St. Louis, where he hoped he would be able to get his monopoly back. But whether he knew it or not —and he probably did—other men had the same idea for their own futures.

The Entrepreneurs

When the Lewis and Clark expedition wintered at St. Louis on its way into the West, it was a fat time for the established merchants there. None of them was as eager to profit from the explorers' needs as Manuel Lisa, a Spanish-American from New Orleans who had made himself relatively rich running a trading post among the Osage Indians. He had originally been given that right by the Spanish grandees, and he kept his job after the Louisiana Territory passed into French hands. He may have spent the rest of his life out there among the Osages in Western Missouri if the American government hadn't bought the territory from the French, which he took as a signal that the time had come for him to move on to bigger things.

By the time Lisa got to St. Louis, he knew that his future was in the fur trade. That was clearly where the big money was, and he had all of the qualifications. He was already one of the most successful businessmen on the frontier, an expert in dealing with the Native American tribes there, and he was at home in the unexplored wilderness. Most important, Manuel Lisa was a man who couldn't sit still.

Even as Lewis and Clark were still out in the wild, Lisa went to work collecting every penny that was owed him and lining up partners to help him finance a scheme that that was already fully developed in his mind. By the spring of 1807— less than six months after the government's explorers passed through on their way back to civilization— he had formed the Missouri Fur Company and set it in motion, pushing up the Missouri River with two keelboats packed with trade goods and

Above: Manuel Lisa dreamed of becoming as rich as Astor, and formed the Missouri Fur Company to help him do so.

Opposite page: The Yellow-stone River, one of the sights which must have inspired early explorers.

Below: Shipments of furs were moved by boat at this time, and all trading posts were built on navigable waterways.

Both on these pages: The building of Fort Manuel, Lisa's first fort, on the confluence of the Yellowstone and the Bighorn Rivers. It was designed to allow easy and secure interchange between the Indians, Lisa's trappers and Lisa himself, who lived and worked, at the fort.

about fifty traders and trappers. Some of these men had crossed the mountains with Lewis and Clark and found themselves out of work after their enlistments were over.

Up until that time, dealers had always relied on Native Americans to collect their furs for them, but Manuel Lisa had a better idea. His ultimate plan was to build a string of trading posts that would supply trappers who would be on his own payroll; he established the first of them, Fort Raymond, near the point where the Yellowstone River meets the Bighorn. He named it for his son, but the men who worked for him needed a name they could recognize, and it soon became known as Fort Manuel. It was the first trading post in the upper Missouri country, and it would eventually become his base of operations.

Like the dozens of other trading posts that would follow, Fort Manuel was built to protect the traders from Native American attack, though its main purpose was to make it easier to trade with the tribes. Essentially, it was neutral ground. Behind the stockade was a large barracks area for trappers and travelers, as well as a blacksmith shop and presses for re-bundling the pelts. A three-room structure served as living quarters and office space for Lisa and his partners, as well as honored guests such as Sacagawea, the Indian woman who had guided the Lewis and Clark Expedition. She was to die there in 1812.

Fort Manuel was at the center of Crow territory, and although Lisa intended to eventually cut the Indians out of the equation, he needed their help at the beginning, and as a backstop in the event of lean years later on. His better-financed second expedition the following year established three more trading posts in the area. Lisa used these posts not only to serve other tribes, but to buy the influence he needed to keep the river free of Indian interference so that he could use it as a shipping route between St. Louis and the interior.

There were good pickings a few days up the river from Council Bluffs, but Manuel Lisa had his hopes set on better ones in the virgin country further on. But he had never been up there himself, and he wasn't sure what to expect. He must

Above: Meriwether Lewis posing as a trapper.

have thought he had been sent a gift from heaven when one of his boats crossed paths with a canoe manned by John Colter, another Lewis and Clark veteran, who was well-known to most of Lisa's crew. Manuel Lisa had a reputation for his hard-nosed, no-nonsense approach to everything he did; but, when the occasion called for it, he could charm the birds from the trees. This was one of those occasions.

When the keelboats shoved off again the next morning, John Colter was aboard one of them as the chief guide of the Missouri Fur Company. At the end of the season, the main party went back to St. Louis to distribute their profits and regroup for the even larger exploring party heading out the following spring. Most of the trappers stayed behind, including Andrew Henry, one of the company's major stockholders, who led a party of thirty-two men into the Montana wilderness to explore the area around the Three Forks of the Missouri River. They built a fort there between the Jefferson and Madison Rivers, but they probably would have been smarter to keep right on going. The Blackfeet met them with spears and scalping knives in a series of attacks, and by the time the fort was finally burned down the following summer, twenty of the

Right: Forts, such as Fort Manuel Lisa, provided shelter for occupations like boatbuilding. It was vital to provide enough vessels to transport the hides back to St Louis.

In 1832, Captain Bonneville led a party of explorers into the Rockies.

He was to spend that winter in very harsh conditions.

Right: Manuel Lisa understood the need for good relations with the Indian population. Nothing stood in the way of the trapper like hostile natives.

men had lost their lives protecting thirty packs of beaver skins — about a ton of pelts — worth in the neighborhood of $6,000. That translates to almost $66,000 in twenty-first-century dollars, but everyone involved agreed that the price in lives had been far too steep, and the company's partners decided to redirect their search to the south and west.

Henry led his men across the Continental Divide in 1811, and while they found the trapping even better among the creeks near the Snake River than it had been around Three Forks, they also found the Western Slope environment much more forbidding, and the Blackfoot threat more intense. The venture was a dismal failure, and the Missouri Fur Company was out of business before the end of the year. But Manuel Lisa was a man with a sacred mission. By spring, he had formed a brand new company under the old name, and had sent out another expedition to gather more furs. His previous explorations suggested that Lewis and Clark's estimate of the beaver population in the mountains had been an understatement; having established friendly relations with the Crow and Teton Dakota Sioux Indians, Lisa was fairly sure that he was well on his way to becoming as rich as John Jacob Astor himself.

Apparently Manuel Lisa didn't read newspapers, or he would have known that his adopted country had just gone to war with England. They were his enemies, too, of course (or at least their Hudson's Bay and North West Company minions were), but what affected him more personally was that the market value of beaver pelts dropped like a stone; from $4.00 a pound to $2.50. To make matters worse, the war shut down the port of New Orleans, which made it more expensive to ship pelts to the East.

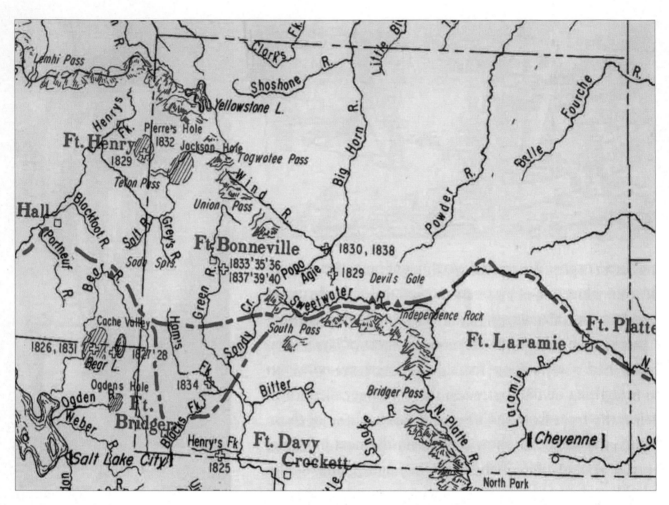

Above: A map by Leroy R. Hafen which documents forts, passes, parks and holes, principal trails, and Rendezvous sites.

Opposite page: The Yellowstone River, which was the site of Lisa's first fort.

In the meantime, the English trappers up in Canada were showing their patriotism by stoking anger among the Blackfoot Indians toward American traders. Still, Lisa and his men soldiered on, staying out of the way of Blackfoot warriors and concentrating on trading with tribes that didn't hate them quite as much. He confined his efforts to the upper Missouri, until he died eight years later in 1820. The Missouri Fur Company went on without him, and with very little change in the way it operated.

The company did renew its efforts to penetrate Blackfoot country. They tried again in the fall of 1821, when Michael Immell and Robert Jones led one-hundred and eighty company trappers — the biggest force yet — right into the lions' den. A short time afterward, the two leaders and nine of their men were ambushed by Blackfeet, who scalped five of them and left the rest for dead. All of their traps, horses, and a whole season's worth of pelts were carried off, and the company

decided that it was time to revert to its policy of avoidance. This saved lives, but it cut profits, too, and within another year the Missouri Fur Company was no more.

The dream went on, though. Competition had been a thorn in Manuel Lisa's side for years, and it became far more intense under his successors. Among their rivals was the St. Louis-based French Fur Company, which became first among equals in the territory below the Cheyenne River but it met its match when the Columbia Fur Company established itself in the Dakotas. Columbia was a formidable operation, run by a team of highly experienced men who had lost their jobs when the North West Company merged back into the Hudson's Bay empire. But there were others — smaller but no less aggressive— out there nipping at their heels; and all the while Astor's American Fur Company was quietly biding its time, waiting to take over after the groundwork had been laid by less conservative adventurers.

Among the men eager to blaze that trail was William Ashley, who formed a partnership with Andrew Henry, one of Manuel Lisa's star trappers, in 1822, hoping to thrive where the others were only surviving. Ashley wasn't a trapper himself, but he knew that he could make money from them. In his detachment, he was able to stand back and figure out what others were doing wrong, then order changes with nothing but a steady eye on the bottom line.

Ashley had gone west from Virginia twenty years earlier, before making a substantial fortune operating lead and saltpeter mines in Missouri. He became a brigadier general in the army during the War of 1812, which incidentally was a shot in the arm for his mining enterprise. When Missouri became a state nine years later, he was elected its lieutenant governor. Although the mountains were full of trappers by then, and some of them were fairly sure that the British dream of creating a beaver desert had been accomplished. Ashley knew that the richest territory lay in Blackfoot country, and that it was still virtually untouched. Getting there was at the heart of his business plan. As it happened, there was another tribe waiting to be heard from out there.

Opposite page: One of the most hostile tribes that the mountain men faced was the Arikara, close cousins of the Pawnee. Here is Bear's Belly, clad head to foot in a grizzly bear skin, presumably one that he has personally taken from its original owner.

Below: Indians brought their collections of hides to the fort, where they could trade them for guns, beads, and other supplies.

Right: William Ashley joined up with Andrew Henry, one of Manuel Lisa's star trappers, and kept a pet bear.

The Ashley-Henry Company did surprisingly well at first, most notably establishing its base of operations at Fort Henry near the junction of the Yellowstone and Missouri Rivers. But before they could celebrate their good fortune, two of their supply boats were ambushed by Native Americans, leaving fourteen dead and the Ashley-Henry dream a shambles.

The perpetrators in this case were not the dreaded Blackfeet, but the Arikara, close cousins of the Pawnee, who were nursing a special kind of hatred for white men in general and Americans in particular. The trappers called them "Rikarees," or just plain "Rees." In earlier times they had been among the friendliest of the Western tribes, and their fondness for Spanish and French trade goods prompted them to establish themselves as emissaries to their more suspicious neighbors. But the traders also brought them smallpox, and the tribe was nearly wiped out in the mid-eighteenth century.

Above: Rocky Mountain vista in spring. The beauty of the country belies its harsh side, where man must struggle to survive.

Right: Ashley's strategy was to avoid main waterways where Indians lurked, waiting to attack and rob unwary trappers. He sent parties of trappers overland on horseback with packmules.

When the Arikara chief died on his way east to a pow-wow with the American President Washington, the Arikara blamed the Americans. To make matters worse, when American hunters arrived on the scene twenty-five years later, they cut the Arikara out of the loop; the tribe's hatred of Americans—already a near-religious obsession—intensified further. It came to an ugly head with the attack on the Ashley party, but it didn't end there.

The next step was a retaliatory raid by American troops led by Colonel Henry Leavenworth that levelled the major Arikara villages. It left the tribe scattered and nearly defenseless, worsening their animosity. And if there was one thing the American trappers didn't need, it was another hostile tribe to keep them looking over their shoulders.

For his part, Ashley took the massacre as a sign; not to get out of the business, but to shift his emphasis from the upper Missouri to the central Rockies. More importantly, he made the precedent-breaking decision to completely abandon the role of the traders and put all of his resources into trapping alone. Others like Manuel

Below: Waterways were still the only way to transport hides from the forts and trading posts.

Lisa had been flirting with that idea for years, but the basic time-honored system of trading furs for goods among the Indians always won out in the end. But with no background in the business,

Ashley saw that the cost of trade goods didn't always square with the price of the pelts, and the Indians weren't always all that eager to go out and produce the kind of numbers he needed to keep his profits and losses in line.

Within a few months of the Arikara attack, Ashley sent an expedition into the Rockies to start putting his plan into action. It was led by Jedediah Smith, Tom Fitzpatrick, and Bill Sublette, who— although they didn't know it at the time—were the first of the new breed that would be forever remembered as mountain men.

Belowt: A scene from the Ashley camp in 1825 showing the variety of characters that gathered in the mountains. The man on the right is Ogden, a representative of the Hudson's Bay Company, who sold Ashley a large consignment of pelts at a bargain rate, which rescued Ashley from bankruptcy.

Key to Ashley's strategy was avoiding the traditional river routes in and out of the interior and sending trapping parties overland on horseback instead. Mule trains trailed behind them with provisions and were also used to transport their bounty. His predecessors had fielded large parties in hopes that a show of strength would make the Indians think twice about attacking them, but Ashley's men fanned out in pairs or three-man parties to gain the advantage of stealth. Their instructions were to explore and set traps on their own, and to meet at the end of the summer at a specified place where they could sell their furs to the company and buy fresh supplies from it. The first of these gatherings, which became the annual Rendezvous, was held in the summer of 1825 at Henry's Fork of the Green River in the southwest corner of Wyoming, not far above the Utah border.

The following year they met in the Cache Valley near Hyrum, Utah, and by the time it was over, William Ashley had become the richest man in the Intermountain West. The Rendezvous became an annual event after that, with the mountain men gathering at various prearranged locations every year (except 1831, when the supply train got lost) until 1840, and—at least in the early years—each gathering was more profitable than the last.

Ashley himself bowed out and gave up the fur business after the second Rendezvous. He had built up a substantial war chest to campaign for Congress, and he went on to serve three terms in Washington as a member of the House of Representatives, where his experience watching his back in the mountains must have served him quite well. The business was sold to its top producing men, Jed Smith, Bill Sublette, and Dave Jackson, each of whom had long-since become legendary in their own right. But Ashley was still their silent partner and advisor. His influence in Washington counter-balanced Astor's lobbyists, who had been the only game in town when it came to dictating the government's fur-trapping laws.

Above: Re-enactors display authentic hand woven horse livery, as used by Native Americans.

The Summer Rendezvous

Below: Rendezvous sites have been preserved and marked for visitors to enjoy. This site is in Riverton, and dates to 1838.

William Ashley established the summer Rendezvous as a way of gathering together his trappers, giving them a chance to sell their furs to the company and buy fresh supplies from it. It cunningly combined business with pleasure and it is probable that much of the money that the trappers saw for their years work found its way back into the Ashley-Henry's company coffers in exchange for drink and supplies. However, nobody seemed to mind, and the event prospered until 1840.

Right: Two women dressed in the clothing of the 1830s walk to a recreated Rendezvous in the Northern Rockies.

Below: Ashley was the first to establish the summer Rendezvous on a large scale as a method of conducting the fur trade.

Top and bottom left: Rendezvous were always held near a water supply, like Horse Creek in 1833, and Riverton in 1830.

Above: In 1834, the Summer Rendezvous included several different camps within ten miles of each other, upstream of the confluence of Ham's Fork and Black's Fork.

Colter's Hell

Opposite page: Geysers
in Yellowstone National
Park, where John Colter
thought he was in hell.

Below: Yellowstone Falls in
Yellowstone National Park
are a breathtaking feature
of this dramatic landscape.

"Legendary" is a word that comes up time and again in descriptions of individual mountain men, and many of these legends are actually true. But the most unbelievable yarns told in the winter mountain camps were usually about John Colter. Everyone who knew him swore that he was the least likely of anyone among them to exaggerate his adventures, but he stopped telling his own tales early in the game because nobody believed them.

They couldn't be blamed for snickering when he told them about steaming water spouts spewing out of the ground, of ponds so boiling hot that you could cook a fish in them, of hot mud that made unearthly sounds when it bubbled up to the surface, grotesque formations of brilliantly colored rock, glass mountains, and trees that had turned to stone. Not even the Indians talked about things like that, and no white man had ever seen them except for John Colter, who we know now

Right: A pair of fine powder horns. Such supplies were gifted to Colter by Lewis and Clark when he agreed to join Hancock and Dixon for a two-year trapping expedition.

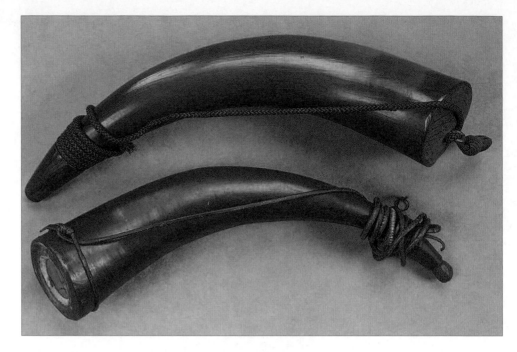

was the first white man to see the fantastic landscapes of what would become Yellowstone National Park.

When Meriwether Lewis and William Clark set recruitment standards for their exploration of the West, they described their ideal candidates as "good hunters, stout, healthy, unmarried men accustomed to the woods and capable of bearing bodily fatigue in a pretty considerable degree." It was a fairly good description of the mountain men who followed in their tracks and a perfect description of John Colter, who joined their party as a private in the fall of 1803 at a salary of five dollars a week. Colter was a thirty-year-old Virginian who had grown up on a farm and mastered the art of woodsmanship as a boy. Later, he turned his back on civilization by migrating to the frontier.

He spent his first winter as a member of the expedition in a kind of boot camp that had been set up across the Mississippi River from St. Louis. The camp was designed to turn civilians like him into soldiers and toughen them up to face the unforgiving wilderness ahead. Colter was more than ready to face just about any challenge by the time the training period was over, and he was assigned to the crew of one of the keelboats that started up the Missouri the following May. It wasn't very long before his skills as a marksman earned him a promotion to hunter, and his forays away from the main party in search of game proved that his skills as an explorer were even more valuable.

On the eastward return journey, Colter also attracted the attention of his superiors with his ability to handle a canoe. When the party split in two, he went with Lewis's group up to the head of the Jefferson River to retrieve the boats they had hidden there. They paddled the boats down to the Great Falls of the Missouri, where he added to his reputation by shooting the rapids rather than guiding his craft through the white water with ropes as all the others resorted to doing.

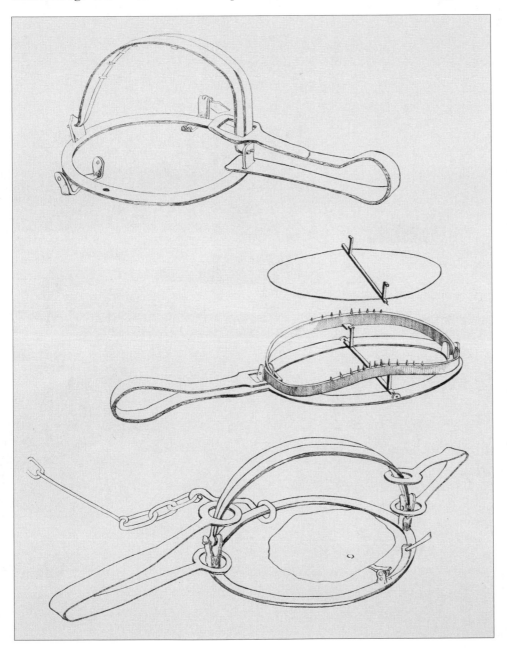

Left: Colter supplied traps for the project, which he funded using his back pay from the Lewis and Clark expedition.

Just before the two parties regrouped along the Missouri River, Lewis met up with two hunters camped along the riverbank— the first white men he had seen since he left St. Louis— and invited them into his camp. They said their names were Forrest Hancock and Joseph Dixon, and that they had been hunting and trapping beaver in the area for nearly two years. They hadn't accumulated as many pelts as they would have liked, but the fact that their scalps were still intact seemed to be a minor miracle. Even more miraculous was their attitude; they didn't have the slightest intention of giving up, they said, and if they could trouble Lewis and Clark for a bit of ammunition and some other basic supplies, they were eager to get out and set some more beaver traps. After this request was granted, they followed up with another, explaining that their outlook would be very much improved if they could acquire a third partner from among the ranks of the explorers. This was against army regulations, of course, but with the end in sight, Captain Clark was in an expansive mood, and when Colter asked him for permission to join the two men and stay in the wilderness, Clark granted it. This was provided that the rest of his men understood that this was an exception, and wouldn't ask to be separated until after they arrived back in St. Louis.

For his part in the enterprise, Colter agreed to furnish the beaver traps, which he paid for out of his back pay. It was further agreed that payment for the other supplies would be made in the form of beaver skins when they all got back to civilization. In one of the early examples

Left: Sulfur Springs conjured up images of fire and brimstone, reinforcing Colter's perception of Yellowstone as a hellish landscape. Later, many openly laughed at Colter's descriptions.

Below: Hot springs, which may well have contributed to "Colter's Hell."

of casting off surplus army gear, expedition officers and men sweetened the pot with small gifts of utensils, powder horns, knives, and hatchets, and other things that could help make life a whole lot easier over the two years Colter predicted it would take for him to earn a fortune. Along with that, the stake included twenty traps, tools for building shelters and canoes, and a two-year supply of powder and shot. Lewis and Clark's men had been encouraged to keep diaries, but although it is believed that Colter was able to read and write, he wasn't among the ones who took the trouble. The result is that the time between the day he left the party and went off on his trapping adventure until he reappeared alone on the Missouri eight months later is a blank slate. Both of his partners were experienced trappers, and it's that Colter learned most of the tricks of the trade from them and through his

own hands-on experience over that time. But it was an otherwise unproductive experience, and it ended with a falling out between the partners, who went their separate ways, leading Colter to his fateful meeting with Manuel Lisa.

By signing on with the professional trapper, he consigned himself to six long years completely out of contact with the civilized world. When Lisa built his fort on the Yellowstone River in the midst of Crow country, he was also counting on being able to attract other tribes to trade with him. Many, including the Sioux, the Shoshone, and even the Blackfeet usually went into that area for the winter buffalo hunt; but if the Crow were friendly to the whites, the other tribes weren't friendly with them. The only way to make the post a going concern was to get the word of its existence out to scattered Crow winter camps and to reach their friendlier neighbors. As far as Manuel Lisa could see, there was only one man qualified for the job, and that was John Colter. Neither of them had any inkling what a monumental undertaking it was going to turn out to be.

Above: Lewis and Clark. President Jefferson appointed a young army captain, Meriwether Lewis, to organize an expedition up the Missouri River in 1803. Lewis requested that his former commanding officer, William Clark, be appointed to accompany him. The journey took eighteen months; they sighted the Pacific on November 18th, 1805, having traversed the breadth of continent.

Right: The Tetons and Teton Basin. Colter definitely tracked through this area during his five-hundred-mile trek. He walked part of this journey backwards so he could recognize landmarks on his return journey. This was a widely-used mountain man technique.

Above: Trappers were right to be extremely wary of tribes like the Blackfoot, and it was often better to steer clear of them entirely. John Colter seemed to be on a collision course with them.

Wearing a thirty-pound pack of equipment, supplies, and trade goods, and carrying a rifle, Colter set out on foot in the dead of winter, following a southwesterly course that took him first to the North Fork of the Shoshone River—which the Crow called "Stinking Water"— near where Cody, Wyoming, is today, and which was the site of a Crow settlement of about a thousand back then. Colter's map existed only in his head, and experts still debate where he went from there, but it is believed that he climbed to the top of one of the nearby mountains to have a look around and figure out where he would be likely to find clients for Lisa's fort.

It is probable that he went on across the eight-thousand-foot Snowshoe Pass to the Wapiti Meadows and into the Big Horn Mountains, where he probably struck off further west in the direction of the rugged Hoodoo Mountains over in Idaho before heading in the general direction of Lake Yellowstone. It added up to a tough challenge in any kind of weather, and it is regarded even today as virtually impossible in winter. But then, John Colter was no ordinary man; he wasn't even a run-of-the-mill mountain man.

As anyone who has ever visited this section of the Rockies knows, after you've struggled over one mountain, you're likely to find another even more forbidding peak rising up beyond it. But Colter didn't think of the mountains as obstacles so much as landmarks that would guide him on his way back, and he pressed on. This attitude was the stock in trade of mountain explorers; some were even known to walk backwards part of the time so that they'd recognize the territory when they were coming from the other direction.

Colter's accounts of what turned out to be a slog of five-hundred or more miles over forbidding, unexplored country were mostly unbelievable, even though others who followed much later corroborated his claims. But what stuck in everybody's craw were his descriptions of the geysers, sulfur springs, and other thermal features he had seen. They began to refer to the land he describe as "Colter's Hell." Surely the old man had come unhinged in the wilderness, they thought. It was no wonder, considering what he must have been through.

We now know that such things are common in modern-day Yellowstone Park, though modern researchers who are still attempting to pinpoint Colter's actual route suggest that he may not have entered the geyser basins there at all, rather skirting them over the tops of the surrounding mountains. After ranging down into Wyoming and through Jackson Hole and the Teton Basin, he turned north again, following Indian game trails in the direction of his home base. But while those trails crossed directly through the future park's territory, they carefully avoided going anywhere near the geysers and steaming rivers, which frightened the Native Americans who had forged the trails. They wouldn't even talk about them, but John Colter did—even if he may have only seen the spectacle from a distance.

It is also possible that Colter's Hell wasn't Yellowstone Park after all, but rather the country up along the Shoshone River. That area is rather benign today in terms of extraordinary geological features, since a huge portion of it is hidden by the massive reservoir behind Buffalo Bill Dam, built there in 1910. But before the reservoir was built, records indicate the existence of tar pits and an extensive sulfur industry there. Either way, though no one can say exactly what route he actually followed, there is no denying that John Colter truly believed that he had seen a preview of hell itself. After all, who in the world could invent such fantastic sights?

By the time Colter got back to Fort Manuel by following the Yellowstone River, Manuel Lisa and his men had long since given up any hope of seeing him again. As a kind of reward for his efforts, Manuel Lisa made Colter a free trapper; but that didn't mean that he didn't have further plans for him.

For some mysterious reason, the Blackfeet in the region had initially left Lisa's men alone. They weren't exactly passing around the peace-pipe, but they didn't seem bent on driving the newcomers away, either, and Lisa couldn't help wondering if they might have finally resigned themselves to the white man's presence. If that were the case, it would be good news for his fur company, but he needed to be sure; so, in the early summer, he asked John Colter to visit the Blackfoot village in an effort to better understand their thinking. Colter had recovered from his five-hundred-mile walk by then and was restless for more adventure, and he told Lisa that he'd combine the mission with a trapping excursion he was already planning up the Gallatin River.

He wasn't in any particular hurry to meet the Blackfeet face to face, and Colter spent most of the summer visiting old friends and making new ones among the Crow Indians, and running lines of beaver traps. He was on his way back to the fort when he first encountered the Blackfeet, but it was far from the kind of meeting he had been anticipating.

He and a couple of Crow guides were paddling down the river when they found themselves in the midst of a fearsome battle that was raging between some fifteen-hundred Blackfeet and about half as many Crow and Flathead. Colter and crew pulled ashore and joined the fight, but Colter took an arrow in the leg. Unable to stand, Colter retreated into the brush, firing the whole time. Eventually the Blackfeet cut and ran. But the fat was in the fire; Colter's presence on the battlefield had been noticed, and he became Public Enemy Number One among the Blackfeet.

After his wound had healed, Colter set out again with a partner named John Potts to run some traps along the Jefferson River. A few days into the trip, they were taken by surprise when hundreds of Blackfeet suddenly appeared along both banks and motioned for them to come ashore. Seeing no other choice, Colter steered the canoe onto the bank.

As it touched the shore, one of the Indians grabbed Potts's rifle. Colter pulled it back and tossed it over to his partner, who was still in the boat. Potts fired it as he was shoving off again, killing one of the attackers, but he was cut down by a hail of arrows for his trouble. And that left John Colter all alone at the mercy of a band of furious Indians. The Blackfoot language doesn't have a word for mercy, though, and although he didn't have any idea what might be in store for him, Colter was pretty sure that it wasn't going to be an easy death.

They gave him a kind of preview by hacking Potts's body into little pieces, throwing them one by one in Colter's face. Then they stripped him naked, all the while deciding among themselves what the most entertaining way to kill him would be. They were setting Colter up as a target for their spears and arrows when their chief came up with a more creative idea.

He led the white man out about four hundred yards onto the prairie, and told him to start running for his life. Then, he signaled his braves to try to catch up with the fleeing captive. Colter knew that his four-hundred-yard lead didn't amount to

Below: One of the Indians grabbed Potts's rifle.

much; when the Indians took away his clothes, they also took his moccasins. He was naked under the blazing sun, barefoot on ground littered with sharp-edged prickly pears. Still, in a race for life, creature comforts are the last thing a man thinks about, and Colter gave it his best shot.

The plain ran unbroken for about six miles before it reached the relative safety of the Madison River. Colter had run about half the distance before he gathered up enough courage to look back over his shoulder. What he saw was a disorganized mob of enemy Blackfeet, all apparently so certain they'd be able to catch up with him that they didn't seem to be trying very hard. The gulf between them and their prey had widened, with one exception: one brave armed with a spear was well ahead of the others, about a hundred yards behind Colter.

Realizing that he might have a chance after all, Colter pushed himself to run even faster. But the exertion caused his nose to bleed, and by the time he was about

a mile from the river the upper part of his body was covered with blood. Meanwhile, he could hear the footfalls of the nearby brave closing in behind him, and he braced himself for the burning sensation that he knew would come when the spear was hurled into his back. In his desperation, he suddenly turned around and held out his hands to meet his attacker head-on.

The Indian was taken by surprise; not only by the gesture, but by the bloody appearance of his target. More that that he was exhausted, and the exertion of trying to throw his spear caused him to fall to the ground. In that split second, in spite of his own exhaustion, Colter was able to grab the spear and plunge it into the brave's chest. Then he grabbed the spear and the Indian's blanket, bolting off in yet another burst of speed to the river, arriving well ahead of the horde of Blackfeet.

He dived into the river and swam a mile or so until he came to a small island, where he discovered a mass of floating driftwood that had piled up during the spring thaw. He knew that, if his luck didn't run out, this could be his salvation. Positioning himself under the pile of wood, with only his nostrils above the water, he was finally able to relax for the first time that afternoon. But he knew that he wasn't out of the woods yet. The Indians were already on the riverbank, and their war cries were beginning to sound furious. They searched everywhere, even on the island where Colter was hiding. Eventually they moved on, their angry chatter fading into the distance. Colter stayed in his underwater hideout until after sunset, at which point he swam quietly down the river for another mile or two before going ashore and setting out on foot in the direction of the fort, which he knew was a hard seven-day slog away.

His most obvious escape route was through the mountain pass at the end of the Gallatin Valley, but Colter figured that the Indians knew that as well as he did, and so he opted to scale the near-vertical walls of the mountain instead. The ascent took him all night, and he rested on the mountaintop for much of the next day before scaling down the other side after sunset.

Opposite page: A sensational magazine depiction of John Colter's harrowing ordeal with the Blackfoot Indians. Such stories fueled popular fiction for over a century.

Above: A rather fanciful illustration from the same 1950s magazine article, depicting an incident during Colter's "amazing adventure."

Above: Daniel Boone escorts settlers through the Cumberland Gap in the Appalachian Mountains. This painting is by George Caleb Bingham (1811 – 1879). The work was painted between 1851 and 1852.

The rest of the journey brought Colter out across the open plain. He covered the distance walking night and day, stopping only for catnaps and to gather roots and bark, which passed for food along the way. By the time he reached the safety of the fort, no one there recognized the gaunt bearded man standing in front of them. But at least he had escaped with his life, and if anybody should have been cured of any inclination to go back into Blackfoot country, it certainly should have been John Colter.

But Colter wasn't a quitter. He had lost his traps in the Blackfoot ordeal and was determined to go back and retrieve them. He waited until winter set in, figuring that the Blackfeet would all have moved into their winter camps. As it turned out, he figured wrong. He passed into the valley again and set up camp along the riverbank, where he made the uncharacteristic mistake of building a fire to cook his dinner. Even before the buffalo steak was seared, he heard bullets whining around him, and he was off and running for his life once more, over the same ground he had covered back in the fall. Once again he avoided the canyon and scaled the mountain to the plain beyond, retracing his route back to the fort. This time he swore that he'd never go back into Blackfoot country again, no matter what. His luck had been pushed to the limit.

But Colter hadn't gone to all that trouble just for the adventure of it. He was still determined to make some money, and when a party headed out for the Mandan Villages on the Missouri River with that year's catch, Colter went along with them. He lived among the Indians in their big lodges until fall, when he agreed to lead another expedition into the Three Forks area— Blackfoot territory yet again. This time, however, it wasn't the Indians but the weather that would prove to be his biggest challenge. A blizzard struck as they were crossing through Bozeman's Pass, with snow amassing in great drifts that the explorers swore were sixty feet deep. It took them a whole day to cover just four miles, and when the sun came out again, John Colter was hopelessly lost. After a day or so of searching, he was finally able to pick up the trail along the Gallatin River, but there were signs of Indians all over the place. And even if there hadn't been any, Colter's imagination was full of awful memories.

A few weeks later back at the fort, he reaffirmed his vow never to enter Blackfoot land, gave up his association with Manuel Lisa, started building a canoe, and made arrangements to join a party that was headed for St. Louis.At this stage of his life, Colter couldn't cope with living in a town as large and bustling as St. Louis had become, and he settled on a farm about sixty miles west of the city, on the south bank of the Missouri River. Just having a permanent roof over his head must have been a foreign experience for the storied outdoorsman.

By an incredible coincidence, one of his nearest neighbours was Daniel Boone, a legendary explorer himself. Boone had blazed the trail for the Wilderness Road through the Cumberland Gap in Kentucky more than thirty-five years before, and had opened the Allegheny Mountains for the country's first westward expansion. He had also survived a one-hundred-sixty-mile trek through unexplored country after escaping from the clutches of the Shawnee. It would have been fascinating to eavesdrop on the stories these two adventurers must have told one another; but, like so much else in Colter's life, these discussions went unrecorded.

Old Gabe

Above: What is believed to be the only surviving photograph of Jim Bridger.

Even considering that the average American had a life expectancy of thirty-nine back in the early nineteenth century, it may seem strange that when eighteen-year-old Jim Bridger went up into the mountains, his new friends started calling him "Old Jim." In fact, the word "old" seems to have been attached to the names of a host of trappers of all ages, possibly as in "good old." In Bridger's case, it may also have been because he was the kind of enterprising young man that General Ashley had advertised for, ambitious beyond his years.

Jim had been orphaned at fourteen with a little sister to look after, so he went to work piloting a ferryboat across the Mississippi into St. Louis. He then became an apprentice to a local blacksmith, an experience that not only taught him a valuable trade, but gave him insight into the finer points of horse trading, which was the blacksmith's profitable sideline.

The roster had already been filled when Jim attempted to sign on with Ashley's outfit, but he appealed directly to Andrew Henry, who was impressed with his eagerness and bent the rules to sign him up. This gave him a special responsibility to live up to the boss's confidence, and although he was one of the youngest in the party, he had a mature outlook and a work ethic that might have put the most experienced among them to shame— if any of them ever stopped to think about such things, that is.

Jim Bridger was an unusually friendly guy. He liked everybody he came in contact with, and everybody apparently liked him even more. He was a natural leader, and when Jed Smith, his booshway (a company field boss who hired and supervised trappers) was asked to evaluate him, he wrote that Jim had all the skills of the angel Gabriel. Jim still wasn't very old, and he certainly didn't look much like anybody's idea of an angel, but from that moment on he was known as "Old Gabe" for the rest of his life.

He was up on the Yellowstone when Ashley's supply boats were attacked by the Arikara hundreds of miles down the Missouri. When word reached the camp,

Left: Jedediah Smith was Jim Bridger's booshway, or field boss, and is seen here in his epic crossing of the Mojave Desert with a party of mountain men. It was the toughness and tenacity of the mountain men that made them great explorers over all terrains.

Above: Jedediah Smith signed on with Ashley's 1822 expedition to the Upper Missouri River. A year later, Smith led another group into the Central Rockies, rediscovering Wyoming's forgotten South Pass. This was crucial to the settlement of Oregon and California.

Andrew Henry organized a party to go down and help, and Jim was picked to go along. They couldn't recover the lost supplies, of course, but they needed to put the Indians in their place to keep an outrage like that from ever happening again. The only way they could get the message across to the Arikara was by overcoming them in battle. Fortunately for the trapper band, they were joined by Colonel Leavenworth and his Sixth Cavalry, as well as five-hundred Sioux warriors itching for a fight. The mountain men, Bridger among them, were mustered into the army as privates. By the time they marched on the Arikara, the expanded army and its Sioux allies had them outnumbered by better than two to one.

The Sioux led the first wave of the attack but were thrown back; once the troops (who called themselves the Missouri Legion) moved in, however, it was the Arikara who retreated. Following the accepted rules of engagement, Leavenworth ordered an artillery bombardment. Shells flew all afternoon, until the powder ran out, but no real damage was done; the Arikara had managed to slip out of their villages during the bombing and were now safely out of range. They climbed the hillsides and shouted insults at the white men.

For their part, the Sioux were just plain disgusted. This was the first time the horse soldiers had battled the Indians, and, to the Sioux at least, it seemed to have been a big waste of time. This was no way to fight a battle as far as they were concerned, and they concluded that the vaunted cavalry was about as threatening as a bunch of old ladies, and that no Indian had reason to fear them. The mountain men serving with the white soldiers couldn't have agreed more, and when the battle appeared to be over they joined the Sioux, who refused to smoke the peace pipe. This amounted to insubordination, since the mountain men were newly-minted members of the military. They took their disobedience one step further by burning the main Arikara village to the ground before hightailing it back west. If the army had proven to be a paper tiger, the Indians got the message that the mountain men most certainly were not.

Old Gabe got his first taste of real Indian fighting on the way back to camp, when he and his team were repeatedly attacked. He found the battles thrilling, but he hadn't signed on to beat back hostiles —though he would be called on to do plenty of that in his new career. He became a free trapper not long afterward when his three-year contract with Ashley expired, and in a season or two he was bringing in more pelts by far than any other man in the outfit. Even though he was no longer bound to Ashley-Henry by contract, he went right on selling his pelts to the company and building cash credits to support his sister back in St. Louis.

Opposite page and below: A beaver dam (left) and beaver pond (below). Jim Bridger was renowned for his skills in seeking out beaver. "Every last mountain man knew how to decimate a beaver colony, but only a born explorer could lead them to one."

Left: In the landscape of
the Rockies and Tetons,
Old Gabe could
instinctively evaluate
which areas were most
likely to yield results.

Above: The landscape that the mountain men encountered was largely one of expansive lakes and swift flowing rivers – enclosed on all sides by pine trees and the distant prospect of sharp-peeked mountains.

But independence had a price. As a company man, finding beaver had always been someone else's job; all he was expected to do was trap them. But now it was up to him to track down their hidden dens, an impossible task without at least one other man. Jim wasn't the only man who was faced with this predicament, so he called on his reputation for reliability and fairness to strike a bargain with some of the other free trappers. He organized them into brigades; they would maintain their independence, although someone would have to be in charge of coordinating their efforts. Though the venture was his idea, Jim faced stiff competition for the leadership role. Other trappers were more experienced, though Jim could usually at least match their skill. It soon became apparent that he had one important quality that none of them came even close to matching: Old Gabe was without any question the best explorer who had ever come into the mountains. Every last one of the mountain men knew how to decimate a beaver colony, but only a born explorer could lead them to one.

Nothing escaped Jim's eye, and he was single-minded about listening to the descriptions of the terrain that other mountain men offered and remembering every word. He also hung on every word the Indians spoke over their campfires, and when the Crow told him of a trail that would lead to lush beaver country on the other side of the mountains, he followed it and discovered the elusive South Pass.

The South Pass is a twenty-mile gap in the Continental Divide through the Wind River Mountains of central Wyoming. His discovery opened up a bonanza for other trappers, and it would later prove crucial to the Pony Express and to those travelling the Oregon Trail. Dozens of others have taken credit for making the discovery— and considering what it meant to the growth of the country, it's no wonder. Of course, considering its size, somebody would certainly have stumbled on it sooner or later. But at the very least, Old Gabe was the first to show others the way across.

The pass is at the end of the Sweetwater valley, and it is marked by a granite monolith rising up three hundred feet from the plain. It eventually became known as Independence Rock, and marked the halfway point between the frontiers of American settlement and the new land beyond the mountains. Almost no one who passed it could resist the urge to carve his name on the sheer rock face, and the graffiti now memorializes hundreds of mountain men who passed that way.

When the trappers gathered for the 1826 Rendezvous in the Cache Valley on the western side of the pass, the conversation among the mountain men turned to the question of where the Big Bear River might lead. Old Gabe was elected to find out, and he built himself a bullboat out of fresh buffalo skins and green willow sticks. After shooting the rapids in the narrow canyon, he climbed a mountain to see what he could see; what he spied was a huge body of water. He climbed back into his boat and pushed on another twenty-five miles until he got to it. He was amazed that the boat rode much higher in the water there, and he was even more surprised to find out that that the water was too salty to drink. He hiked back up to the Rendezvous site to tell his cronies, who concluded that he must have found a shortcut to the Pacific Ocean. But Old Gabe was smarter than that, and after heading back to the valley for a second look at his discovery, he decided he would

Below: A bullboat could be fairly rapidly constructed using green willow sticks and fresh buffalo hides. This could be used to shoot the rapids or cross a deep river.

call it the Great Salt Lake. Jim Bridger always considered that to be his greatest discovery. He considered the lake to be his and his alone, since he alone had discovered it. This would lead to bad blood between Jim and the Mormons when they came along and claimed it as their Promised Land, but until then the valley was all his, and he loved every square foot of it.

Although Jim had developed a powerful dislike for the military during the Arikara skirmish, he was impressed by their discipline, and he adopted many of their policies as his own once he was running his own outfit of trappers. The fiercely independent men who regarded themselves as his equals didn't much like his idea of daily inspections — they resented any kind of authority, in fact — but with the orders coming from Old Gabe, it just seemed natural to let him have his way. His organized approach made Bridger's men the most productive brigade in the mountains. It also served them well in their non-stop encounters with the Indians and their ever-present competition. It's hard to say which was more life-threatening.

In 1832, the Rendezvous was held at Pierre's Hole on the Idaho side of the Grand Tetons near the headwaters of the Snake River. It was quite likely the most perfect spot the Company ever chose for its annual fair. A valley thirty miles long and in places half as wide, with wide grassy plains to forage their horses, plenty of

Below: The 1832 Rendezvous at Pierre's Hole called for the construction of a stockade to ward off attack from Gros Ventres.

good water, and timber enough to feed their fires and to build forts if they had to. They would have done well to build a stockade, because before the fun was over the mountain men would find themselves in the thick of the biggest battle any of them had ever fought together.

The trading went quickly that year and after less than a week, the men had sobered up enough to begin moving on. They had clues that there would be trouble on the trail. The company supply train led by co-owner Bill Sublette had been attacked by Blackfeet on the way in and they had barely escaped with their lives, let alone their wagonloads of trade goods. Tom Fitzpatrick, too, had been attacked, and he limped into the Hole with nothing but the clothes on his back.

There were maybe three hundred trappers there when he arrived, along with several hundred friendly Flatheads and Nez Perces, and he was glad for the safety in numbers. But the numbers began to dwindle when Milton Sublette led a party

Far right: Blackfeet and Gros Ventres plagued trappers and supply trains to the Rendezvous in 1832. Tom Fitzpatrick limped back into Pierre's Hole with nothing but the clothes on his back.

of some thirty trappers in the direction of the Snake River country. His band also included about a dozen inexperienced men recently arrived from the East, and a group of Flathead men, women, and children looking for protection. They hadn't gone eight miles when their fears were justified.

The Indians who attacked were not Blackfeet, but Gros Ventres, a prairie tribe so closely allied with them that few mountain men bothered to make the distinction, even though the Gros Ventres were far more warlike. They were notorious horse thieves and were on their way back from an unsuccessful rustling raid on the Arapaho when they stumbled upon the Rendezvous. When they spotted the isolated camp, they moved in for the kill.

They came screaming down from the hills, about one-hundred-fifty of them, and then stopped just out of rifle range of the camp. When their chief rode forward with a peace pipe, the trappers all knew it was a trick, but one of their leaders rode out to meet him anyway with a Flathead brave at his side. The chief held out his right hand as a sign of peace, but the white man grabbed it and held on, and then he shouted an order to his Flathead companion to fire.

The chief slumped over dead in his saddle, and his people ducked for cover. The mountain men took cover themselves in a ravine, and bullets whizzed back and forth all afternoon across the no-man's land between them. A couple of the mountain men rode out in a wide arc around the battlefield back to the Rendezvous site in a dash for help. Jim Bridger was the first to respond. Leaving a small party behind to guard the camp, he led the rest pell mell to the rescue.

The sight of them drove the Gros Ventres deeper into the brush and the improvised log fort they had built behind it. The mountain men and their Indian allies weren't able to see them, but they themselves were making easy targets, and charging the hostiles was out of the question. Two or three of the men had made the attempt and died trying. Bridger kept up the pressure by ordering his men to

Above: Winter camp. It was important to hole up for the winter to conserve supplies and protect horses and equipment.

keep firing and he managed to get the enemy's makeshift fort surrounded. But it was still a standoff, so he ordered the Indian women and children to start gathering brush so they could burn the enemy out. But the enemy wasn't going to take that lying down. Their leader shouted that they were all ready to die and that riders had already been sent out calling on the Blackfeet to come avenge them. The Gros Ventre language was quite different from the tongues of the mountain tribes, and when the listeners tried to translate the words, they became confused. But to most ears the message was clear: the Blackfeet were on their way to attack the Rendezvous site. If they weren't stopped, the mountain men stood to lose everything they had worked for a whole year to accumulate. More important, more than a few of them had left their Indian wives and children back there.

Bridger and the others broke off the battle right away and raced back to Pierre's Hole, but when they got there, they found a peaceful scene. There hadn't been any attack and there was no sign of any Indian movement anywhere nearby. They waited until dawn, the traditional time for an Indian attack, but when none came it slowly sunk in that they had been tricked. They raced back to the battlefield but, of course, the enemy had melted away by then. The trick had worked.

Old Gabe and his outfit headed north after that, bound for the Three Forks area where the beaver were still plentiful. During one of several skirmishes with the Blackfeet along the way, Jim took two arrows in his back; one of his men tried to pull them out when they got back to camp, but neither of them would budge, and Old Gabe had to resort to what they called butchering them out. This involved widening the wound with a sharp knife, then probing for the arrowhead under the flesh. He was able to get one of them out this way, but the other was wedged in there and no amount of painful cutting and tugging could make it budge. He settled for removing the shaft, leaving the three-inch iron point where it was.

Old Gabe went right back to his trapping as though nothing had happened, and then he and his men went into winter camp. But they weren't happy campers. It had not been a good year. The Native Americans had become more troublesome than ever, and the competition more cutthroat. Even the winter weather seemed to be conspiring against them, and they had to relocate their camp

Above: The ruin of a trapper's log cabin very similar to the one shown opposite.

in the face of a blinding snowstorm so their horses wouldn't starve to death — a fate that the men too were facing. Unfortunately, they left an easy trail for the Blackfeet to follow, and when their new camp was attacked, most of their supplies and all of their horses were stolen. If there was anything good to be said about that winter, it was that Kit Carson, who was making a name for himself as a trapper and Indian fighter, joined Old Gabe and some of his men when they went out to reclaim their stuff. But even that expert help wasn't enough. The Indians routed them and drove them into the cover of some brush, where they laid low through a long freezing night without a fire.

But there was no use crying over spilled milk, and come spring the brigade fanned out again to trap some more beaver and try to cover their losses. Bridger used some of the time to buy new horses from the Nez Perce, but they, too, were stolen, this time by a band of Arikara. Still, by the time they showed up for the Rendezvous, which was held that summer on the Green River just beyond South Pass, Old Gabe's outfit had more packs of beaver to sell than any of the others (even if it a was depressingly meager inventory); and every brigade, like their own, was woefully short on horses.

Right: A fine painting by William de la Montagne Cary of Jim Bridger with Sir William Drummond Stewart. The Scottish nobleman was a crack shot who loved life with the mountain men.

Right: Sir William Drummond Stewart attended the 1833 Rendezvous. A Scottish Baronet with a taste for adventure, he shared his ample provisions of Scotch whisky with the mountain men, with riotous results.

It had obviously been a bad year for all of them, but the Rendezvous was a time for having fun, and this time the three-hundred grizzled trappers had something to make fun of. Among the visitors that year was Sir William Drummond Stewart, a Scottish baronet who was on a Wild West version of an African safari. He wore white hunting jackets and plaid trousers, and topped off the ensemble with a crisp Panama hat. His entourage included a retinue of servants and a well-stocked larder with wagon-loads of hams and other dried meat, preserves and pickles and a very good selection of fine wines. He dined in style from tables with white tablecloths and sipped brandy over the campfire until it was time for bed, not an Indian blanket spread on the ground, but a real mattress covered with blankets of the finest Scottish wool.

But for all that, Stewart's skill with a rifle was a match for any mountain man, and he had given an excellent account of himself during a small Indian raid. He was friendlier even than Old Gabe himself, and he generously shared his stores with all of them. It was probably the first time in their lives that any of these mountaineers ever tasted Scotch whisky. It certainly was the first time that their drinks weren't watered-down during a Rendezvous.

The distraction was a bright spot in an otherwise terrible year for most of them. But the season that followed was even worse, and now the Crow were beginning to grumble about what they considered the one-sidedness of their alliance with the whites. The business was also being threatened by a new law that prohibited whiskey in Indian country, and that would make trading a bigger problem for the mountain men, who still desperately needed horses.

Jim Bridger took a Blackfoot arrow in his back in 1832 and lived with it until it was cut out by missionary Marcus Whitman at Fort Laramie a year later. Iron arrows of this kind were still in use by hostile tribes at the time, but were gradually replaced by trade muskets.

In the meantime, the Hudson's Bay Company opened a trading post on the Snake River, bringing the British and their old tricks back into the area. Astor's American Fur Company was spreading out by then, riding roughshod over all the others, and the Rocky Mountain Fur Company went out of business, leaving Bridger and his men without a friendly customer. Jim responded by forming his own company and buying the trading post at Fort Laramie as its headquarters. It was the first real home he'd had in more than a dozen years, and to make it a domestic success, he negotiated with a Flathead chief for his daughter, who became Bridger's bride. Even better, a missionary named Marcus Whitman was camped nearby, and when Old Gabe found out that he had been a surgeon, he hired him to cut out the old arrowhead that had been buried in his shoulder for three years. It was a long and painful operation that provided an afternoon's entertainment for his neighbours, who came from far and wide to watch. It also did wonders for the reputations of both Jim and the doctor, and left Old Gabe feeling frisky again.

He ran traps during each of the next four seasons, often in the territory that became Yellowstone National Park. But the Indians made his life miserable, and his unscrupulous competitors kept his spirits on edge. When everyone gathered for the 1837 Rendezvous on the Wind River, he found it as quiet and depressing as a

Right: Fort Laramie still exists and much work has been done to restore it. Jim Bridger owned a share in the fort for a while. When he grew tired of trapping, he decided to concentrate on trading with the settlers who passed his way. This view shows the settler's store, where Jim Bridger turned a penny or two in his favor.

winter camp. In their lust for profit, the trappers had even begun taking immature kits from the dwindling beaver colonies, and it was obvious to anyone who took the time to think about it that there was no future in beaver trapping anymore, at least not in the central Rockies.

Shortages often result in higher prices, but not here. A beaver pelt was fetching less than half as much as before. But Jim loved that country more than any man alive, and moving on wasn't an option for him. He was thirty-five years old and left with nothing but memories. They were good memories, to be sure, but a man had

Above: The Lander Cutoff sign which spells out a sinister message. Jim Bridger advised many of the passing immigrants, including the Mormons, on how to navigate the hazardous mountain crossing.

Right: Fort Laramie in the early days. All of the forts started out as wooden structures but were gradually replaced with brick buildings, becoming less fortified over time as the Indians became less of a threat.

to eat. Besides, he had a daughter now who he had shipped off to school in Oregon, so he also had tuition to pay. His Indian wife didn't need much, but he still had to take care of her, and he had also been supporting his sister and her family back in St. Louis. These things hadn't been a problem before, but now everything was beginning to look different.

He revisited his old haunts over the next couple of years, but he found them all lonelier than they had been in their prime. Fortunately, there were better days ahead. He still owned an interest in the trading post at Fort Laramie, and he suddenly realized that that was where the future was waiting. On his trips down to the fort, Bridger had often met up with emigrants bound for Oregon. He was always impressed by their spunk and by their determination not to turn around at this final point of no return. No amount of warning about the dangers ahead could keep them from going on, and some of his old pals from the trapping days were building second careers guiding them over the mountains. But although he generally liked the emigrants and even admired many of them, leading greenhorns by the hand through mountain passes and around Indian camps wasn't his idea of fun. Besides, he had a better idea.

Old Gabe was a master blacksmith, and he was the savviest horse trader west of the Mississippi. He also knew everything there was to know about this strange country, and he was completely open about sharing everything he knew. He was like everybody's Dutch uncle, never skipping over the unpleasant details, but always enthusiastic about the positive ones, and everybody who talked with him came away thinking that he was their best friend. It was no act. Old Gabe really was as honest as Abe Lincoln and as friendly as a bear cub, but his charm also made him richer than all of his years as a beaver trapper had, and he didn't even have to get his feet wet.

Faced with the prospect of climbing the mountains ahead, he made the Easterners understand that grass was going to be scarce on the other side, and that their horses would probably starve to death out there. They were usually half-starved already, and their oxen not only had their ribs showing, but their hooves were generally worn down as well. There was no way, Jim warned them, that these animals were going to be able to haul heavy wagons over the steep hills ahead. So

they sold him the wagons and their livestock, too, trading them for healthier pack animals and lighter, more practical loads, and Bridger turned a nice profit on both sides of every transaction. These Oregon-bound emigrants were short on experience and their advance planning had usually been misguided, but they were long on determination and hope, and they usually had plenty of cash. Jim Bridger appears to have been one of the first to notice.

For his next trick, he moved out of Fort Laramie and built a new fort that he named for himself, closer to his beloved mountains, where the trail crossed the

Above: Mountain men often hired out their services to guide wagon trains of settlers across the mountain passes they knew well.

Above: The first waves of settlers entering the Valley of the Great Salt Lake, which Jim Bridger discovered.

Black Fork of the Green River. He included a blacksmith shop where he could shoe the emigrants' horses and repair their broken-down wagons. And following another of his early careers, he established a ferry to get them across the river.

Best of all, as far as Jim was concerned, these wagon trains only passed through during the summer months, and that left him free to do some hunting and trapping and yet more exploring during the rest of the year. If he had died and gone to heaven, Old Gabe couldn't have been a happier man.

But he was also a restless man, and staying in one place for two or three months at a time gave him a nagging case of cabin fever. Trapping season was in the fall and spring, and after his first year as a wagon train trader, he put together yet another brigade, thirty men strong, and headed for the Milk River up above the Missouri in North-central Montana, east of present-day Glacier National Park. It turned out to be an expensive disaster. The Sioux saw to that.

Jim didn't run traps as a business after that, but he spent his free time working with government surveyors who were busily making maps of the region, and he helped plot a shorter road to the west, which just coincidentally ran right past the front door of Fort Bridger. He even spent one season acting as a guide for another foreign sportsman, Sir George Gore from Ireland, who arrived to hunt for bear and bison to add to his exotic trophy collection back home, and was himself every bit as exotic to the old mountain man as Sir William Drummond Stewart had been.

Old Gabe's last years in the mountains were packed with adventure, and came full circle when he was mustered into the army once more as a guide and Indian fighter. He eventually went home to a farm he had bought years earlier in Missouri. He had leased his fort to the government for the last ten years, and now they had turned it into a military reservation, without ever paying a cent of the rent they owed him. It became clear that that they never would once the Mormon Legion burned it to the ground during their strange little bloodless war with the horse soldiers.

Within a short time after his uneasy settling down, Jim Bridger was totally blind. Those eyes that had seen so much wouldn't see anything anymore. He shared

Left: Surviving buildings in Fort Bridger, Wyoming. Located at Blacks Fork on the Green River, this fur trading outpost was established by Jim Bridger in 1842. It became a vital resupply point for wagon trains on the Oregon Trail.

stories of his adventures with his children — he had several of them by then by three different Indian women, all of whom had died — and he sat for long hours facing west, remembering all the amazing things he had seen and done out there. He sat there on his front porch for thirteen more years, apparently too tough to die, until he finally slipped away quietly in 1881, at the ripe old age of seventy-seven, still the undisputed king of the mountain men.

The Stuff of Legends

Jim Bridger was a wet-behind-the-ears eighteen year-old when he first went up the Missouri River, close to being the youngest member of the Ashley-Henry team. One of the oldest was Hugh Glass, a forty-year-old experienced outdoorsman who is *definitely* not remembered as a team player. On their way back from the battle with the Arikara, Andrew Henry issued strict orders for all of the men to stick together to deal with Indian attacks. Glass frequently defied these orders, straying off on his own to do a little hunting or exploring, but mostly to make a show of his independence. He eventually took one too many of those little jaunts. But it wasn't the Blackfeet who brought it to a painful end. It was an entirely different menace, one that always brought terror to the wildest imaginings of every mountain man.

Like most of his colleagues, Old Glass's life before he became a beaver trapper is largely a mystery. But what little he said of it points to an early career as a crew member aboard a pirate ship in the Gulf of Mexico, commanded by the infamous Jean Lafitte. He and one of his shipmates gave up that line of work one night, jumping overboard near the Texas coast and swimming for shore. They headed north, he said, and made it all the way up to Kansas, where they were captured by Pawnee Indians, who had no intention of letting them go any further.

Glass was forced to watch as the Pawnee slowly roasted his partner over a ceremonial fire, watching Glass all the while to gauge his reaction. It was obvious that he was about to meet the same fate — or worse — but he showed no sign of fear, and the Indians interpreted his casual indifference as bravery, the only trait they ever respected. He never explained how or why, but he claimed that on his way up from the coast he had picked up some vermillion, a bright red waterproof dye that was highly valued by the Indians. Apparently certain that he wasn't going to need it where he was going, he offered it as a sort of parting gift to the Pawnee chief, who was hugely impressed by the act of generosity coupled with his apparent fearlessness.

Whether all this was true or not, Glass swore that instead of burning him alive or finding some other way of torturing him to death, the chief made him a blood brother of the tribe and adopted him as his own son. During the year or two that followed, he lived as an Indian, their ways becoming second nature to him. The

Left: A beautifully dressed re-enactor. His costume epitomizes the outfits worn by the mountain men.

Right: Though some of their diet is plant-based, grizzly bears are powerful predators, eating everything from rodents to deer to moose.

Pawnee were the most feared marauders of the plains, and his life as one of them surely must have made his days as a buccaneer on the Spanish Main seem like time spent at a Boy Scout camp.

Glass eventually wound up in St. Louis when the Pawnee chief went there for negotiations with an Indian agent and brought Glass along. His knowledge of the nuances of the English language was invaluable to his adopted father, who showed his gratitude by allowing Glass to stay in the white settlement after the meetings were over. It was there that he joined up with the Ashley-Henry Company.

On his foolish foray away from the main party that day in 1823, he had just hacked his way through a thick tangle of wild plum bushes when he came face-to-face with a massive seven-foot grizzly bear feasting on the plums with a pair of yearling cubs, either one of which was big enough to maim him with a casual swipe of its paw. Like every mountain man, Glass always carried his rifle loaded and ready to fire, but before he could get off a shot, the startled bear grabbed him by the shirt front with sharp, curved claws as long as a man's finger, picked him up, and threw him to the ground like a bag of dirty laundry. Then the bear straddled him and bit a generous chunk of flesh from the upper part of his leg and next it went for his shoulder. When Glass threw up his arms in a futile gesture of defense, the grizzly grabbed them and repeatedly chewed through them one by one, all the way to the bone.

The sound of his terrified yells and the blood-curdling grunts and growls of the angered bear attracted the rest of the party, and when they arrived on the scene the combined force of their rifles brought the animal down and it fell dead, all eight-hundred pounds of it, onto Glass's nearly lifeless body. Yes, Hugh Glass was still alive after all that, but just barely. Nobody expected him to live to see the sunset.

In the all-for-one, one-for-all code of the mountain men, there was nothing for them to do but wait at his side for the moment of death. He would have to have a proper burial out there where scavengers could pick his body clean in no time at all, if Indians didn't desecrate it first.

None of them had any experience with treating and binding wounds, especially ones as fearsome as Glass had suffered. But they did the best they could, then put together a makeshift bed of buffalo robes and willow branches, and moved him into a shaded grove of trees. He lived through the night, but his agonized moaning and groaning was a sign to all of them that he was about to go under — their euphemism for dying — any minute.

Meanwhile, the band had suspended its trapping operations for the battle with the Arikara, and they desperately needed to move on and make up for the lost time. Moving him was completely out of the question, but they couldn't leave Old Glass there alone, either. Andrew Henry called for a pair of volunteers to stay behind and protect the man through his last hours, and then see to it that he had a proper burial. Of course, no one stepped forward to volunteer. There was Indian sign all over the place, and it had just been made painfully obvious to them that they were in grizzly country. Henry solved the problem by asking every man to contribute one dollar that would be given as a bonus to any two among them who would stay behind. There were eighty men in the party, and the incentive of what amounted

Above: A single-springed bear trap. Grizzly pelts were highly valued.

Right: Rivers and water-
ways led the way into the
wilderness. This is Crystal
Creek, Colorado.

to a half-year's pay for a man willing to stand by the dying old man was powerful enough to attract one of the most experienced among them, a trapper remembered only as "Fitzgerald" who stepped forward. The other volunteer was young Jim Bridger, who would eventually make a name for himself in other ways.

Their death watch lasted through two days and nights. Although his condition didn't improve, Old Glass wasn't showing any signs of going under, either. On the third day, Fitzgerald spotted Indians in the near distance and, after a long argument, he finally convinced Jim that they'd surely be dead themselves if they stuck it out. As they prepared to slip away, they took Glass's rifle and his possibles bag, which they would present to the others as evidence that Glass was dead and buried.

Their deception worked when they arrived at the fort, and after a fair fall trapping season, they settled in for the winter at Fort Henry. It gave Jim a chance to sit down and think for the first time, and he didn't like the memories. They were giving him nightmares, and then one night one of them came to life. He thought he was seeing a ghost when a wild-eyed white bearded old man appeared at the fort and grabbed him by the arm. But this was no visitor from the grave; it was a badly mangled Hugh Glass, hungry for revenge. He raised his rifle — Bridger couldn't tell where it had come from — and ordered Jim to explain himself, and quickly.

In the meantime, the commotion brought the others out of their bunks, and when Andrew Henry joined them, he pushed the rifle aside and ordered Glass and Bridger into his quarters to get to the bottom of the confrontation without any bloodshed. Jim confessed everything, happy to get this business off his conscience; but the real question of the night was how the old man had managed to cheat death. When he woke up all alone, Glass told them, he found himself

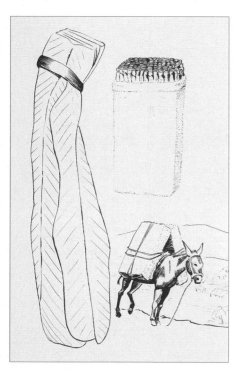

Below: A pack mule loaded with a possibles bag and wads of tobacco, essential tools for most mountain men. Bridger and Fitzgerald robbed these items from Old Glass when they believed him to be dying from a grizzly bear attack.

abandoned with nothing but the buffalo robe that was his makeshift deathbed. Fortunately for him, there was fresh water close at hand, and he was able to creep over to it and to the plum bushes that had brought the grizzly out of hiding.

It took a long time, but the water and the bit of fruit slowly brought his strength back, and then he started to crawl out onto the prairie. He believed that he would find help, not to mention the pair that had done him wrong, at Fort Kiowa, two hundred miles away on the Missouri River, and he was determined to get there

Above: The Indians hunted bears for their meat, their hide, and their strength – some Indians believed that killing a bear transferred its courage and fighting skills to the hunter.

even if he had to crawl all the way. He still wasn't able to stand or walk, but his lust for revenge against Bridger and Fitzgerald kept him going. Luckily he came across a band of Sioux hunters who helped him get to the fort, where he expected to find his betrayers. But both of them had moved on by then, so Glass set out — alone again but now able to walk — for Fort Henry.

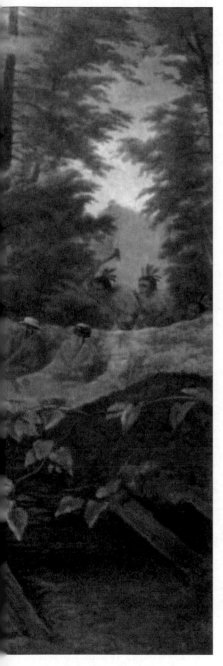

It turned out that he had overheard the debate between the two men over whether or not to abandon him, and he realized that Fitzgerald was the real villain of the piece. He let Jim off with a tongue-lashing that men who overheard it said was the worst any of them had ever experienced. Still determined, Glass took off the next morning in the direction of Council Bluffs, where he expected to find and probably kill Fitzgerald. His sworn enemy was there all right, but he had joined the army in the meantime, and Glass decided that he hadn't walked all those painful hundreds of miles to kill a soldier, which would have probably gotten him hanged. Besides, by then he was thinking that death was too good for Fitzgerald anyway. After another furious lecture and a meeting with Fitzgerald's commanding officer, who promised to see to the proper discipline, Glass went back to trapping, apparently satisfied that justice had been done even at such a terrible price. He was killed the following year by a band of Arikara.

The story of Old Glass and the grizzly was told and retold over mountain campfires for a long time after that, the way most of the mountain man legends were kept alive. But every now and then, some of them told their own stories to newspaper reporters and authors who carried them to the outside world.

One such figure was Jim Beckwourth, who charmed T.D. Bonner into writing a book she called Life and Adventures of James P. Beckwourth, which caused a sensation when it appeared in 1856. But this was no ordinary adventure yarn. It read more like a Victorian novel, artfully combining sex and violence, just the way Beckwourth described it.

In the days before the Civil War, there were very few black men in the mountains, except for the occasional slave brought through no choice of his own.

Left: The Ashley Henry party (which included young Jim Bridger) spent a lot of time fighting the Arikara, one of the most warlike tribes in the area.

Below: An encounter with Indians leads to a capture... or will the trapper dispatch the fallen warrior with his pistol? Life for the mountain man was full of such drama.

But Jim Beckwourth was the son of a slave and a white Virginia planter. He himself had been sold as a slave to a Missouri blacksmith, but he escaped after knocking his master on the head with an iron bar. After that, there was no place for him to run but into the mountains, and he took to the trapper's life like a duck to water. His career as an Indian trader was even more gratifying. He jumped into that life trading with the Blackfeet, about as unlikely a job as any man would want. The Blackfeet were proud of their fierce reputation, and they knew that any outsider who was willing to come among them had to be uncommonly brave. He didn't let them down. Whenever the tribe went on the warpath, Jim was right there alongside them, and he always gave a good account of himself.

When he went off into the mountains, he left the love of his life behind, with the intention to return one day and marry her. But that day was far off, and when one of the Blackfoot chiefs offered him his daughter as a bride, he accepted with enthusiasm. It was fated to be a short but happy marriage. Although he had a powerful reputation as a fighter among the Indians, he never joined them when their raids were on the white trappers, whom he regarded as his own people. When one party rode back into camp with white scalps, he refused to join them in their

Jim Beckwourth with plains rifle.

Opposite page: Blackfoot warrior in ceremonial clothes. The Blackfeet were a proud people with a reputation for being fierce fighters. Beckwourth moved amongst them fearlessly, which gained him much respect.

scalp dance, and he ordered his wife to do the same. But while the festivities were in full swing, a friend told him that he ought to come out of his tent and take a look, because his wife was putting on the show of her life out there, dancing and celebrating with the rest of the party. Furious, he forced his way through the crowd, marched up to his dancing wife, and hit her on the head with the side of his tomahawk.

She appeared to be dead, and a cry went up among the crowd that he should pay for this outrage with his own life. But his father-in-law, the chief, came to his rescue. In his speech, he acknowledged his grief at losing a daughter, but he pointed out that she deserved to die because she had disobeyed her husband, a worse crime than murder — even unjustified murder — among the Blackfeet. It is a husband's right to take the life of a disobedient wife, he reminded them, and almost before the message sank in, he offered another of his daughters, younger and handsomer than the first, to become Beckwourth's second wife.

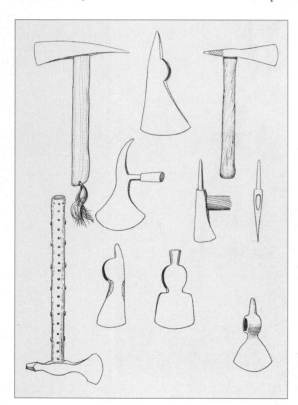

Above: Various tomahawk styles. Though considered an Indian weapon, most iron examples would have been made by white blacksmiths and traded with the Indians.

The first one recovered a few days later, and now Jim had two wives, which was perfectly acceptable in Indian society. But he may have seen trouble ahead, and in a month or so he left the Blackfoot village and carried about three-dozen beaver packs into Fort Henry. He was careful to send back gifts to his wives and their father the chief, as if to say that they wouldn't be seeing him again any time soon.

Although Beckwourth was a fairly productive trapper, General Ashley considered him more valuable as an emissary to the Indians, and he sent him out among the Crow. Even though an enemy Blackfoot chief was his father-in-law twice over, the Crow accepted him into their ranks because of a story a previous Ashley representative had invented about Beckwourth, one so outlandish that the Crow believed no one could have made it up.

The story was that Beckwourth was actually the son of a Crow chief, who had been kidnapped by the Cheyenne as a boy and had now grown into a fearless warrior. The Crow chief's wife was suspicious. Her son had in fact been captured in this way twenty years earlier. She would believe that this was her long-lost child, she said, only if she found a telltale mole on his eyelid. By an odd stroke of fate, Beckwourth happened to have just such a mole, and he was welcomed "home"

Above: Jim Beckwourth was a larger than life mountain man who married into the Blackfoot tribe and aspired to Indian heritage, claiming to be the son of a Crow chief. In truth, he was the son of a slave and a white Virginia planter.

with great celebration. The festivities went on for several days, and ended with the chief's offer of a choice of one of his three daughters as his wife. Beckwourth certainly didn't have any objection to that, and he picked the oldest, not because she was the prettiest but because she had the prettiest name, Still Water.

The imitation Indian became a warrior leader of the Crow over the next several years leading their braves to victory after victory with his exceptional horsemanship, his skill with a rifle, and his incredible bravery. His fame was like a license to steal, and he routinely sent horses loaded with beaver packs back to Fort Henry to be credited to his personal account.

In his spare time, Jim pursued further romantic adventures. Before very long he had eight wives, each in a separate lodge, and he had his eyes on two others, both of whom resisted his advances. One of them waved him off because she was already the wife of a chief, but he still didn't give up, and after her husband had him flogged on three different occasions (which produced no sign of cooling Beckwourth's ardor), the chief was finally convinced that the only way to put a stop to this courtship was to allow the woman to become Jim's ninth wife.

But he wasn't finished yet. As was probably predictable, keeping all those wives happy and fighting the tribes' battles was beginning to make Jim a little weary. He announced that he was planning to go back to the white man's world, but one of the maidens he had thought he'd lost came forward and agreed to marry him if he would only stay with the tribe, where he was needed. Jim decided that he wasn't as weary as he had thought after all and accepted her proposition. But five days after the wedding, he set off on a "business trip" to St. Louis, and never went back to live among the Crow.

Five knives of the distinctive design favored by the mountain men. The middle knife is blacksmith-made in the U.S., and the others are factory-made. Despite the rift with Great Britain, many consumer goods were still routinely imported from there. The second knife from the top is marked Eye Witness Sheffield (England), and the fourth is a Green River Pattern knife, also made in Sheffield. Until American industry kicked in, many weapons continued to be imported from England.

Right: Early explorers used Indian guides and labor to penetrate the waterways. Their boat – the canoe – was adopted by mountain men like Bill Williams, who slept in the shelter of a river bank. The canoe would be tethered by a long length of rawhide, which he could cut and cast off silently downstream at the first sign of trouble.

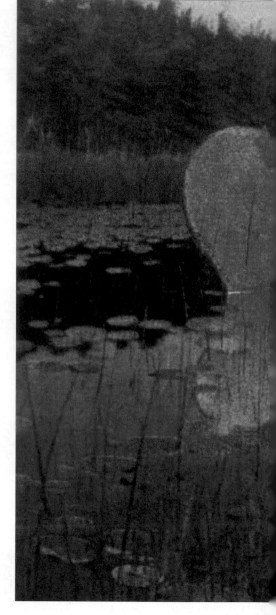

But like others before him, Jim Beckwourth couldn't stay away from the beaver dens. This time he went off into the Southwest where he met and wooed a dark-eyed Spanish beauty and made her his wife, bringing the total, if anybody was keeping count, up to an even dozen. But in spite of his years of experience, wife number twelve didn't find his marital skills up to her expectations, and she left him, taking their daughter along with her. Undaunted, Jim settled down on a Colorado ranch for a life of farming, trapping, and hunting, with a new Indian wife to help see to his needs.

Ironically, he ultimately went back to the Crow villages as an agent for the army to negotiate a peace treaty. He died while he was there, and given a chief's funeral. No Crow chief ever had as many widows weeping and wailing through the long ceremony. Not among them was the girl he had left behind in St. Louis, swearing that she was his one true love. She had grown tired of waiting for him, and had married someone else in the meantime.

If Jim Beckwourth was a kind of social butterfly among the mountain men, Old Bill Williams was his complete opposite, a determined loner. He had gone west as a boy from North Carolina with his head full of the Bible teaching his mother had made her life's work, and by the time he was in his mid-teens, he struck off on his own as Parson Williams, a circuit-riding self-styled Baptist preacher. It eventually took him among the Osage Indians, where he settled down for a while developing a whole new religion that combined his Bible learning with the Indian religion. He became an Osage himself, and even took a wife from among the eligible young women of the tribe; he would marry three of

them before moving on. Bill established a trading post among the Osage in South Dakota, but then he crossed over into Montana to become a trapper. He was welcomed into the mountaineers' camps, but most of them thought he was crazy as a bedbug; he had his own way of doing things, and everything he did seemed to be at odds with their tried-and-true methods. But they admired his skills nevertheless, and he outlasted the best of them, surviving for more than forty years in the wilderness, partly thanks to his odd ways.

Avoidance was at the heart of his method. He nearly always worked alone, to keep from attracting the attention of any Indians who might be lurking about. He always set his traps under cover of darkness, and he worked from a canoe rather than on foot. That way, he was able to glide silently down a stream, putting out his traps as he went along, then he would paddle back the other way in the small hours of the morning, and by the time the sun came up he had retrieved and skinned his catch, ready to spend the rest of the day out of sight. Bill didn't sleep much, but when he did it was usually in his canoe, which he tied to the bank hidden under the thickets of brush there. He used a long piece of rawhide to secure it so that he could easily cut it and float silently away at the first sign of possible trouble.

Williams lived mostly on a diet of beaver meat, even in places where game was plentiful, because he didn't want to call attention to himself by firing his gun to kill an elk or an antelope. But it wasn't as though he wasn't a good shot; he could handle a rifle as well as the best of the mountain men, and in spite of his penchant for solitude, he often joined with others in their fights with the Indians. Indeed, he frequently took charge of such encounters, shouting orders and encouragement to the other men and, of course, outshooting them.

Bill Williams had long red hair and a beard to match; his face was deeply lined and leathery, and he had a long, hooked nose that some said reached all the way down to his protruding chin. He was skinny as a scarecrow, and his voice, on those rare occasions when he used it, was high-pitched and whiny. His friends said that

Below: A two-wheeled cart was useful for carrying provisions for longer expeditions in the wilderness, but cumbersome in mountainous terrain.

they could never tell if he was laughing or crying, although it was a good bet that he never did much of either.

Through most of his later years he rode an old bony horse that he had picked up from the Nez Perce. It looked as though it would never make it over the next hill, but Bill knew better. This animal, ornery as it was most of the time, had as much stamina and iron will as its master. Bill wore oversized iron Mexican spurs whose rowels were decorated with tinkling drops, a strange affectation for a man who relied on stealth, and he rode with his feet encased in huge wooden stirrups that were once described as being "as big as coal scuttles."

His wardrobe never varied; some claimed it was because he hadn't changed his clothes in forty years. His hunting shirt was covered with grease that gave it the sheen of leather, and his slouch-brimmed felt hat was also shiny with grease and the dried blood of hundreds of beavers. His buckskin pants had shrunk over years of wading in streams, and they clung to his skinny legs like a second skin.

When he rode, he was always bent low over his saddle, giving him the appearance of a hunchback. His eyes were always dead ahead, never shifting either left or right; still, he never missed the tiniest detail of the terrain around him. He never looked anyone in the eye, either, and when he talked with someone, his mind always seemed to be a thousand miles away. It may well have been. Bill Williams intimately knew every nook and cranny, every hill and mountain, river and creek for much more than a thousand miles around.

One of the first men to write about the mountaineers was George Frederick Ruxton, an English adventurer who traveled through the Rockies from New Mexico to Colorado, describing his experiences in a non-fiction novel that was published in 1848. Bill Williams was among the characters who added a special spice to it.

In one incident that Ruxton recorded, Bill had joined a large party and appointed himself as its guide into unexplored territory, where he claimed he could tell by the run of the ridge in the distance that they would find water and where there was water there would surely be beaver to trap. Bill Williams had a reputation for lunacy, but as Ruxton explained it, "...All felt secure under his charge. His iron frame defied fatigue and, at night, his love for himself and his own animals was

Above: Trade beads were not only worm as an adornment, but were also used for bartering in a tight situation.

Below: Mountain men devouring buffalo meat. Their pants are shrunk to their legs from years of wading in cold streams.

sufficient guarantee that the camp would be well guarded. As he rode ahead, his spurs jingling and thumping against the sides of his old horse at every step, he managed with admirable dexterity to take advantage of the best line of country to follow; avoiding the gullies and canyons and broken ground which would otherwise have impeded his advance. ... In selecting a camping site, he displayed equal skill. Wood, water, and grass began to fill his thoughts toward sundown, and when these three requisites for a camping ground presented themselves, Old Bill

sprang from his saddle. Unpacking his animals in a twinkling, he hobbled them, struck fire and ignited a few chips, lit his pipe and enjoyed himself."

Old Bill didn't stay with that party long. He disappeared on his own for a long stretch of time, coming back unexpectedly to help them fight off a Blackfoot ambush, and then vanishing again into his solitude. Bill Williams believed that that the best way to fight Indians was to avoid them, and only a man on his own could do that.

When the beaver began to thin out in the mountains, Williams decided to find another line of work. At first he became a horse trader, leading other like-minded former mountain men down into the Southwest and the California mountains,

where Spanish mustangs ran wild. On one such trip they rounded up three thousand of them in California, but while they appeared to be wild animals, they did in fact belong to someone. Williams and his men were forced to race back across the desert with a posse on their heels. The Californians were able to recover about half their herd, but the prices the rest fetched in Colorado made it all seem worthwhile.

Williams didn't normally have much of a stomach for trouble like that, but a couple of years later he signed on, against his better judgment, as a guide with John Fremont's party of explorers headed for the Rio Grande River down from the Sangre

Above: Bill Williams tried to avoid conflict with the Indians by working alone. Many mountain men, however, went on the offensive when threatened by hostiles.

de Christo Mountains in Colorado to look for a route for a railroad. The trip was a disaster (though it did demonstrate that the area was unsuitable for laying a railroad), but they did manage to make it down to Santa Fe; exhausted, close to starvation, and without their valuable surveying equipment that had been lost back in the mountains.

Williams, who was sixty-two years old by then, was one of the survivors, but his reputation was in a shambles, because Fremont heaped all of the blame on him for the failed expedition. In order to redeem himself — even though his reputation never seemed to matter much to him — Bill volunteered to lead a

Above: A roaring fire formed the center of a mountain man's relaxation time; the group here are enjoying a pipe just as old Bill Williams did.

Far left: Frémont, who blamed Bill Williams for the failure of his railroad surveying expedition to the Sangre de Christo Mountains.

party back over the same route to find the missing equipment. They were able to recover it, but on the way out, Old Bill became the loser in a battle with a band of Ute Indians, the kind that he been carefully avoiding all of his life. He never made it out of the mountains alive. Quite likely, if he had been given a choice, that would have been the end he preferred.

Below: The mountain men needed horses with as much stamina as they had. The animals had to be able to ride over mountain passes on a poor diet of berries and tree bark, travel long stretches without access to fresh water, and out-ride Indian ponies at a moment's notice.

Out of The Mountains

Below: In the 1830s, a mountain man would have been on the lookout for Blackfoot warriors in the mountains of what would later become Glacier National Park. Here, Montana's beautiful Sinopah Mountain is reflected in the clear waters of Two Medicine Lake.

Bill Sublette's name was one to be reckoned with among the mountain men, and so was his younger brother Milton's. More than anyone else, they were the ones who showed the way out of the Rockies into better hunting grounds to the south and to the west.

The Sublette family had migrated west from Kentucky to St. Charles in the Missouri Territory, not far up the Missouri River from St. Louis. Young Bill seemed destined to follow in his father's footsteps as one of the local political movers and shakers, and he began by running for county constable and winning the election. But the lure of the mountains was too strong to resist, and at the age of twenty-three, Bill signed on with the Ashley-Henry outfit and went up the river to become a trapper. His success as a beaver hunter and as a shrewd businessman was recognized after three years—as long as it took an ordinary man to work off his original contract—when General Ashley sold the company to him, along with the highly-regarded and much more experienced Jedediah Smith and the relatively unknown David E. Jackson.

Under the agreement, Ashley turned over all of his merchandise in the mountains at the time for sixteen thousand dollars. Five thousand of that was

Left: A map which reminds us how much of western expansion was made possible by the mountain men. Their tireless exploration in search of beaver opened up all of the main access routes over the mountains.

already owed to Smith from a former partnership with Ashley, but the three new partners pledged to turn over all of the beaver pelts they collected until the debt was paid at the end of the first year. Ashley also agreed to supply them with up to fifteen-thousand dollars worth of trade goods over that same year, creating a further debt that was to be repaid after the next fall trapping season. Ashley formally promised not to supply any other company, and he transferred the contracts of forty-two trappers over to the new enterprise. Most important, he used his influence with business interests in St. Louis and in the East to give the company— now called Smith, Jackson, and Sublette—a trading advantage.

By mid-summer, they had made most of the veteran trappers lieutenants of the individual brigades, and while they were getting organized, the partners were making plans for the years ahead. Sublette and Jackson went north to trade with the Snake, Crow, Flatheads, and Sioux Indian nations, ranging as far west as Oregon.

Right: Yellowstone National Park.

Above: The Grand Teton range, where Sublette and Jackson concentrated their fall hunt.

Smith went off in the opposite direction with a party of explorers. They made their way as far as Mission San Gabriel in California, where they were arrested for poaching but talked their way out of before moving on up the Northwest coast. Their furs had been confiscated by the Mexican authorities, but they stole them back before leaving town. Their actions branded them as outlaws in Mexican territory.

In the meantime, Sublette and Jackson concentrated their fall hunt in the shadow of the Grand Tetons, in the area known as Jackson Hole. This was familiar territory to Dave Jackson, who had given it his name years earlier. Hostile Indians drove them northward from there, and they became the first white men to visit the site of Yellowstone National Park since John Colter first saw it twenty years earlier.

Business was disappointing for the partnership, and after three years they decided that their profits weren't big enough to make it a going concern, and they agreed to disband the company. None of the three had given much thought to their personal futures, though like everyone else they were beginning to think that there wasn't much of a future for anybody in trapping beaver in the Rocky Mountains. Smith and Jackson spoke longingly of settling down on farms, and Sublette was already negotiating for a large tract of land near St. Louis. Their plans, such as they were, moved forward when five experienced trappers—Tom Fitzpatrick, Jim Bridger, Henry Fraeb, Jen Baptiste Gervais, and Bill's brother Milton—offered to buy their company.

When the three partners packed up to head back to Missouri, they took a party of about seventy men, ten wagonloads of pelts, and a herd of cattle. The trip was historic because it was the first to use a large section of the Oregon Trail; by routing his big caravan both into and out of the Snake River country, Sublette proved for the first time that the trail could be crossed by loaded wagons, and there was enough grass along the way to sustain their livestock. It blazed the trail for the thousands of emigrants who would soon be following in his footsteps.

Above: The Sublette wagon train blazed the trail for the countless thousands of emigrants that followed.

But neither Sublette nor Jackson was happy in the harness of retirement, and they formed yet another new partnership to extend their fur trading into the Mexican states through Santa Fe. Armed with letters of recommendation from the governor of Missouri and passports that had been secured for them in Washington by Congressman Ashley, they left for the new El Dorado in the spring of 1831 with eighty-five men and twenty-three mule-drawn wagons. Jed Smith decided to give up his idea of retiring and went along with them, even though there was a price on his head down there. The party was also harried in this unfamiliar territory by Black Feet and Gros Ventres, but the local desert tribes, while not particularly friendly, made it a point to avoid them. Jed Smith managed to escape the clutches of the

Above: Bill Sublette had become a gentleman farmer and merchant back in St.Louis when his old friend Sir William Drummond Stewart visited him for another mountain gambol in 1841.

Mexican authorities, but he wasn't so lucky with the Commanches, who ambushed him near the Cimarron River and killed him.

Except for the unfortunate loss of Jedediah Smith, they reached Santa Fe early in July relatively unscathed. But even though their trading was more lucrative than their competitors', Sublette was disappointed with what he characterized as a "hard luck year," and he dissolved the short-lived partnership. Jackson went over into California to establish a mule-trading business, and Sublette led a caravan of Mexican goods back to St. Louis.

Although Sublette had made up his mind to turn his back on the fur business, a new development back east made him think twice about it. John Jacob Astor had just celebrated his seventieth birthday. At the same time, his charter to do business in the West was about to expire, and Astor wasn't sure that he wanted to renew it. He was well aware that beaver had become an endangered species in the West, and he decided that it was as a good a time as any to retire. He had been quietly buying up Manhattan farmland over the years, and had become the owner of virtually the whole island. He went into the real estate business as his second career, and became known as the "landlord of New York."

Sublette and his current partner Robert Campbell hurried to New York to divide the spoils of Astor's Western fur empire. After a series of secret meetings they put together an agreement promising to give up their operations in the Upper Missouri in exchange for a pledge by the American Fur Company to stand down from the mountain trade for at least a year.

It eliminated Astor's cutthroat competition from the territory south of the Missouri, and that gladdened the hearts of the mountain men who were still operating there. But it was an empty victory; making a living trading in beaver furs was getting harder and harder all the time.

For his part, Bill Sublette decided not to join them in resuming his old line of work, although he did help them with their marketing. To all outward appearances Bill had become a gentleman farmer and merchant. He built a retail emporium in St. Louis, became a director of the Bank of the State of Missouri, and started wearing a suit and tie every day. He became a leader in State Democratic politics, too, but his pride and joy was his farm at Sulphur Springs, just beyond the city limits.

Above: In the 1820s, Robert Campbell, originally from Plumbridge,
County Tyrone, Ireland, was just as famous as Jim Bridger, Jed Smith,
William Sublette, and the other notable mountain men.

He read everything that he could get his hands on about modern farming techniques, and developed his property into a model farming operation, even supporting a prize-winning herd of shorthorn cattle from imported English stock. But there was more. He discovered a rich vein of coal on his land and established a profitable mine that kept the homes of St. Louis warm for many winters. There were also mineral springs on his land, and he developed them into a profitable spa

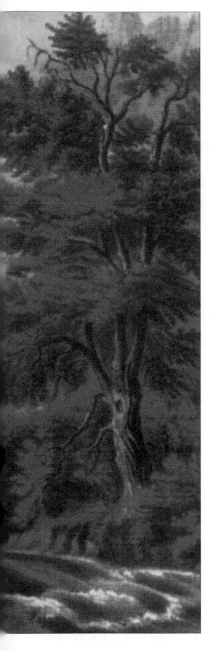

that became a favorite summer destination of St. Louisians who beat a path there to "take the waters."

Bill Sublette was one of the most prominent residents of St. Louis, which was by then a major city. It was the jumping-off point for emigrants heading west. It was also beginning to attract transients who were traveling west not to live there, but to experience the wonders of the mountain country firsthand. Among them was Sir William Drummond Stewart, who had already tasted the experience back when he became the star attraction at the 1833 Green River Rendezvous. Stewart and Sublette had become fast friends back then, and it was he who sparked the trapper's interest in scientific farming and cattle breeding through a long transatlantic correspondence. Now, eight years later, Sir William was back for another hunting and exploring expedition, and Bill Sublette eagerly joined him for what he expected would be a sentimental journey back to his old haunts.

By the time they headed out across the prairie, Stewart had accumulated a large party of "companionable adventurers," including several doctors, a noted botanist, a painter or two, and a couple of military observers, plus a mixed bag of bored, wealthy businessmen from back east. Added to the mix was a pair of musicians from New Orleans, who had been hired to provide entertainment along the way. Stewart outfitted the expedition in the same luxurious style as his previous venture, but Sublette was no slouch when it came to packing luxuries himself. His main contribution came in the form of horses, mules, and wagons, but he also included items like cigars, playing cards, and lots of whiskey.

This was permissible, even though they were entering Indian country, because Stewart had obtained a travel permit that allowed "as much spirituous liquors as he may deem necessary for the use of himself and Party." Sublette obliged by

Left: A romantic view of an oxen-drawn wagon train in a well-manicured wilderness. The Rockies provide a dramatic background.

Below: President James K. Polk whose campaign was actively supported by Bill Sublette and who responded by awarding him the job of Superintendant of Indian Affairs, which he coveted.

ordering a keg of gin, another of rum, and two of cognac. He also packed a dozen bottles of champagne and a good supply of port wine, and if all that wasn't enough, he included a barrel of straight alcohol, just in case the party turned out to be thirstier than he anticipated.

Bill arranged for three mountain men to join them as well as two black slaves, both young boys. All together there were about sixty people in this odd mixed bag of adventurers, a number large enough to avoid any major attacks by Indians. Westward-bound wagon trains were another matter, but the experienced guides were generally able to avoid them.

They slogged on over endless miles through lush valleys and desert stretches, hounded by drenching thunderstorms. They forded unexpectedly swollen rivers and plowed through deep snowdrifts, even though it was already summer. But, as they say, a good time was had by all. By about August, most of the party seemed to have had enough of this mountain gambol, and they started making plans to head back to St. Louis as soon as the leaves began dropping from the willow trees. Despite this, a surprising number of the party seemed determined to keep right on going all the way to Oregon.

For their part, Stewart and Sublette both had business in St. Louis that required their attention - the Baronet had to settle the estate of his recently deceased brother back in Scotland, and Bill was planning to get married. In early September, they turned around for a slow march in the direction of home. They arrived back in St. Louis in November, thoroughly satisfied with their adventure, which had been covered by the press and had made Bill Sublette a kind of national celebrity.

The publicity was good for Bill's political ambitions, and he served in Missouri's Electoral College delegation, which cast its votes for the winning candidate, James K. Polk. Sublette had supported his campaign, even if he had other fish to fry during most of the campaign season. It seemed to give him a leg up for the job of Superintendant of Indian Affairs, but his health was beginning to fail, and managing

his extensive property was also taking a toll. He went east in hopes that the change would be good for his health, but he died the following summer in Pittsburgh, far away from the mountains that he loved.

Newspaper accounts of the Steward-Sublette jaunt through the mountains generally described Bill Sublette as one of the gentleman-adventurers, which by then he had become. His long past days as a mountain trapper were hardly mentioned, although adventures like his were beginning to stir the American imagination, especially among young boys, through the wildly popular "dime novels" that began to appear about that time. By the middle of the nineteenth century, there were enough literate citizens to create a robust market for these books, which mainly concentrated on adventure tales of the sort pioneered by James Fennimore Cooper several years earlier. Without them, few Americans might have ever remembered people like Daniel Boone and Davy Crockett, Buffalo Bill and Wild Bill Hickok. But of all of the folk heroes immortalized by these wild stories, the one who towered above all the rest at the start of the dime novel craze was a mountain man named Kit Carson.

Above: Bill Sublette died in Pittsburgh, far away from the rugged Rocky Mountain passes that he helped to tame.

Below: Kit Carson at the trappers' camp. A highly dramatized illustration featuring the popular image of Kit Carson as explorer and intrepid Indian fighter. He began his illustrious career as a trapper in the early 1830s.

The dozens of books that were written about him were loosely based on his adventures as an explorer and an Indian fighter, but those roles were an outgrowth of his primary occupation: beaver trapper.

Carson seems to have first gotten his feet wet setting beaver traps while traveling with a Rocky Mountain Fur Company brigade in the early 1830s. But long before then, while he was still a teenager, he had gone west along the Santa Fe Trail and made Taos, New Mexico, his home base. By that time, Santa Fe had been a major trading center for decades. Goods brought in over the trail had traditionally been traded for silver until beaver pelts eventually became a more valuable medium of exchange. Some were being shipped down from St. Louis by then, and more were coming down the coast from the Pacific Northwest.

But there was also a strong home-grown beaver-trapping business there, based in Taos. The locals ran their traps in streams around the Colorado River and into Utah, and they were giving the Upper Missouri companies a run for their money.

Young Kit Carson might have been the perfect candidate to join his neighbors on their hunts, but he was repeatedly rejected because he was considered too small, too green, and too inexperienced to survive. This last characterization must have been a case of mistaken identity.

Like Davy Crockett, Christopher Carson was born in the mountains of Tennessee. Raised on the Missouri frontier, "Kit" must surely have had what it took to deal with the rough life of a beaver trapper. After a couple of years of making a living working among the mule skinners and ox drivers along the Santa Fe Trail, he finally got his chance to prove his real worth when a local entrepreneur named Erwin Young signed him up for an expedition he was putting together. Young's intention was to run beaver traps along the Gila River in New Mexico and Arizona.

But their traps stayed in their possibles bags on that trip. When they reached the Salt River in Arizona, they were waylaid by Apaches and forced to hightail it back home to Taos. Young, who had his investment to consider, organized a larger party of some forty men. They turned around and headed back out over the same route, only to run into the same Apache band in the same place where the first attack had taken place. But this time, Young was ready with a plan. He ordered the bulk of his men to hide in a ravine so that the enemy would think they were a smaller, weaker party than they actually were. He allowed the Apache braves into his small camp, but as soon as they crossed the line, he ordered his men to start firing, killing about twenty of them. It was a small victory, though. There were still other Apache bands out there, which launched a series of attacks on the party all along the Colorado River. Once again, the would-be trappers had to turn around and go home empty-handed, their tails between their legs.

Lewis and Clark's Trail

Words and Music by Robert Vaughn

Published by

Robert Vaughn
Great Falls, Montana

Above: In the same way that Kit Carson was singled out as a folk hero by dime novel publishers, Lewis and Clark provided similar inspiration to this Montana-based music publisher. Here the Lewis and Clark Trail is set to music and lyrics by Robert Vaughn.

Below: Indians stealing horses. Carson had to track the thieves for a hundred miles into the Sierra Nevada Mountains to get them back.

But Erwin Young was a determined man. He led his party off in the other direction bound for California, but this turned out to be a profitless venture, too. They arrived at Mission San Jose a few days after a band of Indians had run off and taken refuge among the Miwoks, a tribe regarded as hostiles by the missionaries and the Spanish Californios. They had the Miwok village under siege by the time Young's party arrived, and the pursuers asked the white strangers to help them break the standoff. Young obliged by sending in a dozen men, including Carson, who fought their way into the village and ,after a long day of bloody battling, set fire to it. The following day, they issued an ultimatum promising to leave no Miwok alive unless the fugitives were sent back to the mission. Kit Carson made a name

for himself that day, but as a fearless Indian fighter, not as a beaver trapper. He still hadn't set a single trap.

It was beginning to look as though he never would. Before much longer, another local tribe stole most of the party's horses, and Young sent his new star Indian fighter at the head of a posse to follow their hundred-mile-long trail into the depths of the Sierra Nevada Mountains. One of their animals had been eaten by the thieves before they caught up with them, but they recovered the rest and killed all of the perpetrators, except for a couple of children, who they carried back to begin a new life as mission slaves.

Carson finally got to run some traps after the company laboriously crossed the Mojave Desert again and set up camp along the Colorado River. But he seemed destined never to become a master trapper; Kit Carson seemed to draw Indians to himself like flies to honey. He had been left in charge of the camp with about a half-dozen others when a band of what he estimated to be five-hundred Indians wandered in. They seemed peaceful, but it was apparent that they had weapons hidden under their buffalo robes, and even though the odds were stacked against him, Kit ordered them to turn right around and get out of there or he would start shooting. For some unknown reason, they did as they were ordered, and Kit Carson added another feather to his cap. Not only had he proven to be a fearless Indian fighter, but he had also showed that he had a cool head and could talk his way out of a fight when he had to. But he still didn't have much experience as a trapper, which is what he had signed up for in the first place.

Although Young considered him the most reliable man in his brigade, Kit jumped ship the following spring and joined up with a band of traders from the Rocky Mountain Fur Company on its way back to the Upper Missouri. But he had no intention of signing a contract with that or any other company. He was a free trapper from the start, in spite of his relative lack of experience in running trap lines. He soon established himself in the Jackson Hole country, and then along the Salmon River to the west in Idaho, where he found plenty of beaver and very few hostile Indians. For the most part, he seems to have lived among the friendly tribes and avoided the hordes of Blackfeet and Gros Ventres, and for a little while he managed to live down his reputation as a white warrior.

Ironically, after a year in the Rockies, it was the normally friendly Crow Indians who stole some horses from his brigade's winter camp and brought out the Indian fighter in him again. Several of his companions and two Cheyenne braves followed the rustlers' trail through the snow until they found the Crow camp with their horses tethered outside. They hadn't been spotted, and easily recovered their animals, which should have been the end of it. But a barking dog gave them away, and when the Crows emerged to see what the fuss was about, the trappers opened fire, killing nearly all of them. The lucky ones who got away went to a nearby camp for help and came back with reinforcements. In the meantime, the Cheyennes led the recovered horses back to the white man's camp. Except as an act of revenge, the short fight that followed seemed to have lost its meaning and ended quickly without any more losses. In spite of his sometimes hair-raising adventures in the far West, Carson later recalled this as his first major Indian encounter.

His next, against the Comanche south of the Arkansas River in Colorado the following spring, may have been the most bizarre ever to find its way into any mountain man's book of memories. Kit was travelling along with his partner Levin Michell, the legendary Joe Meek, and three Delaware Indians when they spotted a Comanche war party of about two hundred barrelling down on them across the open plain. Kit Carson and his team were riding mules, which were no match for the fast Indian ponies; there was nothing they could do but make a stand. Preparing for the assault, they cut the throats of their mules and arranged the dead animals in a circle to form a makeshift fort. When the marauders got close enough, Carson's men started shooting in three-man relays so that there wouldn't be any letup in firing while their single-shot rifles were being reloaded. Their marksmanship was outstanding and they made every shot count, but still the odds were hopelessly against them. What did work to their advantage was that the Comanches' horses shied away, and wouldn't carry their riders close enough for hand-to-hand combat because of the strong smell of blood that surrounded the mountain men. It was a standoff, and the Comanche didn't have the patience to wait for the enemy to die of thirst or run out of ammunition. They decided to move on and wait for a better day.

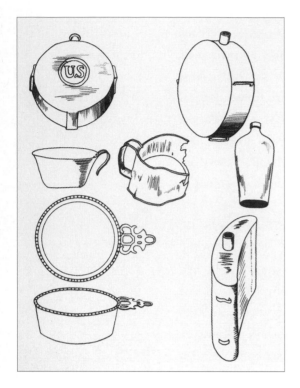

Above: Various types of drinking vessels recovered from mountain men camp sites.

The fact that three members of Carson's party were Delawares wasn't at all unusual, even considering that they belonged to an Eastern tribe. Together with the Shawnee, the Delaware people had been driven out of their original hunting grounds by the growth of European settlements along the Eastern Seaboard, and by the first years of the nineteenth century, the remnants of both tribes had resettled throughout the West. The Indians who were already there—many of them transplants themselves—usually regarded them as white men, since they had adopted some of the settlers' ways before moving west. Chief among these was their skill in handling a rifle, still something quite new in the West. That, combined with their highly-developed battle skills, made them feared by even the most warlike of the plains tribes. And that made them valuable as negotiators between the natives and the white newcomers.

It was only natural that they would travel among the mountain men, sometimes as leaders of white brigades and often forming their own, even though they considered themselves part of proud Indian nations. After all, their people had been trapping beaver to sell to white traders for generations back home, even if it had been in different mountains.

The several nations of the Iroquois had been much more closely associated with beaver trapping back east, and hundreds of them had also relocated west of the Mississippi. In their case, most of them had been transplanted into the upper Rockies and the Pacific Northwest by the Hudson's Bay Company, whose leaders valued them as master beaver trappers. But the Delaware were more common in the central and southern Rockies and, as Kit Carson would testify, they were extremely valuable companions and allies.

After their brush with the Comanche, Carson went on trapping in Colorado for a time, but instead of taking his catch to the next Rendezvous, which would have been far more convenient, he assembled a pack train and set out for Taos, which he apparently thought would be more fun, if not more profitable. He was right on

Below: Mountain men grew adept at building stockades to protect themselves and their horses from Indian attack.

both counts. While he was there he signed up with a party headed back up in the direction of northern Idaho, and after roaming through western Montana pretty much on his own for a year or two, he turned up again at the eventful 1835 Green River Rendezvous.

Among the wildest of the bunch who were assembled there was one of Astor's men, a trapper named Shunar, who Carson later said was "... a large Frenchman, one of those overbearing kind and very strong. He made a practice of whipping any man he was displeased with, and that was nearly all." At one point, Shunar issued a general challenge to the whole camp when he announced that he could beat any Frenchman with his fists, and he could handle any American with a switch. Carson said that he let him "make his brag," and then, ".... I told him that I was the worst American in camp ... and that if he made any more such expressions, I would rip his guts."

That was like waving a red flag in front of a bull. Shunar grabbed a rifle and mounted his horse to ride out for a fight. Carson mounted, too, but instead of a rifle he grabbed a pistol.

Carson's account continues: "[I] demanded if I was the one he intended to shoot. He said no, but at the same time drawing his gun so he could have a fair shot. I was prepared and allowed him to draw his gun. We both fired at the same time; all present said but one report was heard. I shot him through the arm and his ball passed my head, cutting my

hair and the powder burning my eye, the muzzle of his gun being near my head when he fired. During our stay in camp, we had no more bother with this bully Frenchman."

There were many French Canadians in the Rockies by then, following the tradition of their grandfathers, who had been beaver trappers back east. The Indians in the area called them wahkeitcha, meaning "bad medicine", because they found them treacherous and vengeful. But for all that, they feared them much less than the Anglo-Americans who had invaded their territory, who were seen as more daring, if not more open.

Carson stayed in the mountains for seven more years after that, some of the time trapping for the Hudson's Bay Company in Idaho, and some working with Jim Bridger's brigades in Montana, the warzone of Blackfoot country, before eventually joining up with Astor's American Fur Company. There is no indication that he ever met up with his enemy, the bully Shunar, even though they worked for the same company, at least for a time.

Like everyone he did meet in the mountains, Carson knew that the game was over, and in 1842 he decided it was time to pack it in, even though he characterized his years as a beaver trapper as "the happiest days of my life." But, as he dictated

Above: The harsh winter conditions ruled out any opportunity to trap game. This is Montana's Rocky Mountain Front Range. In the 1830s, the area was well known to both mountain men and the Blackfoot Indians.

Above: President James Buchanan, who defeated Frémont in the election of 1856.

for his biography, "it has now been sixteen years I have been in the mountains. The greatest part of that time passed far from the habitations of civilized man, and receiving no food other than that which I could procure with my rifle."

Hundreds of others could have summed up their careers in the same way, but at thirty-two, Kit Carson was still younger than most of them. His future was staring him in the face, but he didn't have a past to fall back on. When he was starting out he had apprenticed as a saddle maker, but he didn't like it at all and ran out on his contract. Apart from that, he had spent his life working at a trade that had suddenly become obsolete. He had never learned to read or write, but he had two young children to support and his own life to maintain. Something had to happen, and quick.

Something did. Kit went back to St. Louis to get his act together, and quite by chance met an army lieutenant named John C. Frémont who, as an officer in the Corps of Topographical Engineers, was organizing a mapping expedition to the Continental Divide and South Pass. He was impressed by Carson's mountain experiences and signed him on as a guide at a salary of a hundred dollars a month, practically a king's ransom to a mountain man.

Frémont's was already a name to be reckoned with after he had led military expeditions to map and explore the Great Plains. He was married to the daughter of Missouri Senator Thomas Hart Benton, a tireless booster of western expansion, and together they sent out reams of press releases to national newspapers, not just to advance their cause, but to keep their own names in the forefront and promote their political careers. Frémont's fame would soon rub off on Kit Carson.

Their first trip into the mountains was relatively uneventful, if one discounts a nasty fracas with the Sioux and the Cheyenne in the Wind River Mountains on the other side of South Pass. But Frémont's publicity machine sent out glowing reports of his own fearless leadership, and never missed any opportunity to credit Kit with plenty of acts of derring-do along the way.

Their next expedition the following year was to connect the territory they had already mapped with the U.S. Navy's survey of the California coast, and in that way to complete the exploration of the entire continent. The journey took them north to Fort Vancouver on the Columbia River and then south through Oregon, down to the Great Basin on the eastern side of the Sierra Nevada. After a rough winter

COL. FREMONT
PLANTING THE AMERICAN STANDARD ON THE ROCKY MOUNTAINS.

Left: Frémont's popular image as The Great Pathfinder rubbed off on Kit Carson.

crossing of the Sierra, they reached Sutter's fort near San Francisco, then turned south through the San Joaquin Valley to the Mojave Desert and back into Southern Nevada and Utah, ending their journey at Bent's Fort in Colorado. The whole trip took a little more than a year, and newspapers kept America well-informed almost every step of the way. They didn't discover much new territory that many of the mountain men hadn't already explored, but thanks to Senator Benton's publicity mill they planted the seeds of the senator's campaign promoting "Manifest Destiny." This was the belief that American settlers had a divinely-inspired mandate to settle the great open spaces of the West. The press was calling Frémont "The Great Pathfinder," and the mountain men who travelled with him, especially Kit Carson, were becoming national heroes. As for Frémont himself, he was pushing his name forward as a possible presidential candidate. He became the first Republican to make the race, in fact, and ended up winning thirty-three percent of the vote in 1856, losing to James Buchanan.

Predictably, the Government Printing Office rushed out copies of now-Captain Frémont's report on his explorations between 1842 and '44. They were self-serving, to be sure, but they were written as lurid adventure tales, and the first printing of ten thousand copies sold out quickly and was followed by several subsequent editions. Kit Carson's name appeared throughout the report as a larger-than-life frontier hero. Most Americans pictured him in their minds as a muscular six-footer in buckskins, with a wild beard and a voice powerful enough to shake the mountains. He was frequently called the American Hercules. But the reality was a good bit different. A few years later, General William T. Sherman sought Carson out, confessing later that he was surprised by the man's true appearance. "[He is] a small stoop-shouldered man with reddish hair, freckled face, soft blue eyes, and nothing to indicate extraordinary courage and daring," the General said. Why, he didn't even have a bushy beard, and his voice was gentle, even calming. No matter; in the public's mind, Kit Carson was no less than the great Hawkeye—James Fennimore Cooper's hero of *The Last of the Mohicans*—in the flesh.

Above: Frémont marched under the Bear Flag into Monterey, where American settlers declared California independent from Mexico.

The image would grow immensely during Frémont's next adventure. The new president, James K. Polk, followed Senator Benton's lead in promoting westward expansion when he welcomed Texas into the Union and started negotiations with Great Britain to annex Oregon as well. But the Mexican government dug in its heels over establishing the borders of Texas and California, and it would eventually take a war to settle the issue.

In the meantime, the President quietly dispatched Frémont on his third expedition. Several mountain men (including Kit Carson, of course) and twelve Delaware Indians joined the seventy-five-man junket. Like the others had been, it was billed as a journey of discovery, but it was obvious to many that Frémont's orders included a search for military routes into California. It wasn't long before California's Mexican Governor came to the same conclusion and ordered the party to turn around and go back where they came from. Instead, they headed north and camped on the banks of the Sacramento River. The anticipated war hadn't yet broken out yet, but the party of explorers took it upon themselves to protect Americans in the area against a horde of Indians—Carson said that there were a thousand of them— who had carried the pre-war skirmishing up from the South. Kit Carson's reputation as an Indian fighter grew by lightyears after a battle he described as "perfect butchery." When it was all over, he said that "[we] had accomplished what we went for and given the Indians such a chastisement that it would be long before they ever again would attack the [American] settlements."

But of course, they had not been sent to fight. As an army officer in a foreign

Opposite page: Frémont by Civil War photographer Matthew Brady.

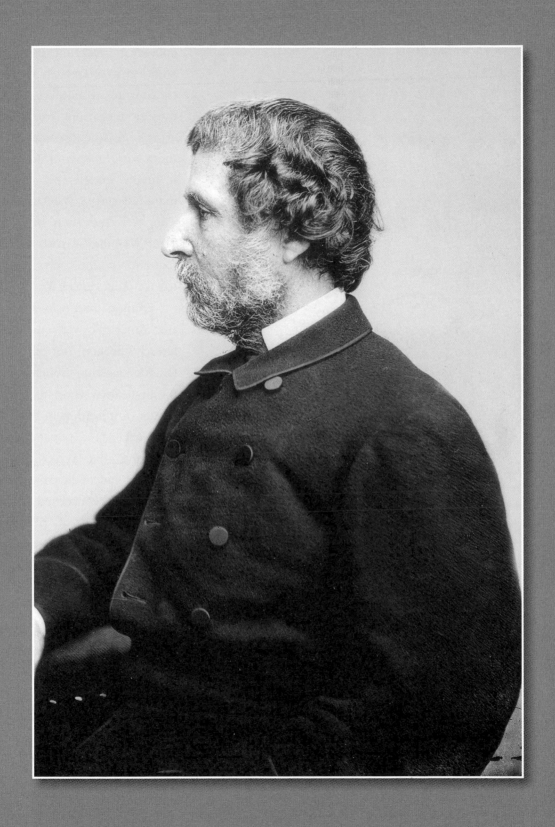

Above: Kit Carson in uniform. President Polk made him an army lieutenant.

country in peacetime, Frémont had no authority to order such a battle. Still he called for volunteers, offering to muster them out from under the army's jurisdiction and then swear them back in when it was over. When it finally ended, he and his men marched across the Oregon border. They were met there by a messenger from Washington with secret orders that Frémont interpreted as a mandate to take California by force.

Frémont had no way of knowing that America's war with Mexico had already broken out along the Rio Grande River and thought he was firing the first salvos when he joined a party of American settlers in launching what they called the "Bear Flag Revolt," declaring that a new independent republic had been created. As far as Frémont was concerned, it was entirely appropriate that his people, who as soldiers and mountain men had paved the way for these Americans to cross the continent, should be on hand to make their declaration of independence a reality.

He and his men rode in triumph into Monterey under the Bear Flag of the settlers who marched as a part of his company. After they easily took the town, the American Navy arrived on the scene shortly afterward, and Commodore Robert Stockton drafted the company into what he called the "Navy Battalion of Mounted Riflemen." He packed them into his ships and transported the men down to San Diego. The town fell quickly, with Los Angeles surrendering at about the same time. The mountain men among them had faced all manner of discomfort during their careers, but none of them had ever experienced a sea voyage before, and all of them swore that they'd never do it again. Getting sick on bad meat was one thing; they knew how to avoid that. Seasickness was something entirely.

Kit Carson was the first to leave Los Angeles when he and a party of fifteen were sent out across the desert in the direction of Washington to deliver a report on the California victory to Senator Benton and the President. They figured that it would take them about sixty days to cross the continent, but fate stepped in when they reached New Mexico. Forces under General Stephen Kearny had just toppled the local Mexican government. When Carson told him about the events in California, he decided to march out there with five companies of dragoons, and ordered Carson to lead the way. The mountain man already had his orders, but General Kearny outranked Frémont, even though he had been promoted to Colonel by then. He had no choice but to entrust the Washington-bound messages to his old friend and fellow mountain man, Tom Fitzpatrick, and head back west.

By the time they got to California everything had changed. Commodore Stockton had declared himself governor with Frémont as his second in command. But the war that had started out so quietly soon erupted into a counter-rebellion. Kearny took charge, but neither Stockton nor Frémont would recognized his authority. As a senior officer, Kearny was able to have Fremont arrested and court-martialed for insubordination.

A short time later, Carson was on his way to Washington again, this time carrying army dispatches. This time he made it all the way, living a life of comparative luxury for a time in Senator Benton's home. He also had two separate meetings with President Polk, who rewarded his service by making him an army lieutenant. Military medals didn't exist in those days, but if they had, he probably would have been awarded the Medal of Honor.

Carson was soon on his way back west, once more carrying messages, but along the way he learned that Frémont had been found guilty at his court-martial and stripped of his rank. He also learned that his own recent promotion had been rescinded in the ensuing backlash. But he felt that had been honored enough by then, and he wasn't so sure he was cut out to be soldier anyway. Back home in New Mexico, the army called upon him time and again to help protect the settlers on the nearby frontier who were now all American citizens. But all Kit Carson really wanted to do was settle down once and for all. His old mentor, John Frémont, had bounced back from his army discharge and become a kind of freelance explorer. After his journey to plot a railroad right-of-way that had cost Old Bill Williams his life, he approached Kit to lead his men on a second attempt before moving with him to California. But Kit was ready to hang up his rifle by then and turned Frémont down. Key to the decision might have been that his Mexican wife of six years was pregnant with their first child. Soon afterward, they moved into the eastern foothills of the Sangre de Cristo Mountains and built a cabin in the grasslands, the Great Plains at their feet and the mountains at their back, an idyllic place for any mountain man to spend his last days.

But if this spot was officially part of the United States, it was also the hunting grounds of the Jicarilla Apaches who, as might be expected, weren't prepared to be neighborly. There were other whites in the region, and they were pleased to have so famous an Indian fighter in their midst. The first dime novel about him, Charles Averill's Kit Carson, Prince of the Fold Hunters, had recently been published and was having selling fast at the local trading post. But under federal law, settlers weren't allowed to fight off Indians themselves but had to call on the military for help. Carson petitioned the governor to authorize civilians to do the job. What he got for his trouble was an appointment to federal Indian Agent, which meant moving back to Taos, since it was against federal policy to allow agencies to be established in Indian country. The government insisted that Indians should take their grievances into the white settlements.

Carson disagreed with most federal policy on the Indian question, and though he considered Taos home, the mountain man in him rebelled against settling down in any town, even one as remote as Taos. But he stuck it out for seven years before resigning in 1861, when a group of Confederate sympathizers staging a demonstration infuriated Carson by raising the Stars and Bars over the main plaza. Union supporters responded by hoisting the Stars and Stripes across the way and posting a twenty-four-hour guard around it. Kit Carson chose to support their cause and rejoin the U.S. Army.

He was promoted the full colonel almost immediately. Although he had technically been an army man under Frémont, he didn't have the slightest notion of how to drill troops. And because he couldn't read or write reports, he was largely in the dark about plans and tactics. Steeped in the individualism of the mountain men, his ideas on military discipline were a full one-hundred-eighty degrees from the West Point men who had qualified to lead. Only did he meet the Confederates in battle, when three regiments of Texas cavalry attempted to take over New Mexico but were ultimately driven back. Still, Carson was made the principal field commander in the area, where the fight was mainly with the Indians—the kind of war that Kit Carson understood very well.

Several other former mountain men were called into service during this Indian war phase of the larger conflict, but they all served as guides. One reason was that

most of them were too old to fight by then; another reason was that they still weren't generally regarded as dutiful citizens by many of their fellow Americans. Kit Carson, on the other hand, was already a national hero, and people were inclined to overlook the fact that he was still pretty rough around the edges. He represented the second generation of mountain trappers (the Lewis and Clark expedition was over long before he was born), and he was a good bit younger than most of the others. But still, he was a fifty-five year-old serving with men who were, on average, ten years younger.

Carson lived up to his reputation as an Indian fighter during those years, most notably in a series of nasty encounters with the Navajo. Even after the War Between the States was over, battles were still raging in the far West. The government's proposed solution to the problem was to cordon off the hostile tribes into reservations. Congress did what Congress has always done: it formed a committee. It sent a delegation out to New Mexico to conduct an investigation into the situation and determine how to resolve it. Their expert witness was Kit Carson, who understood the differences between the individual tribes better than anyone. He recommended that the direct responsibility over the Native Americans ought to be turned over to the War Department rather than the Bureau of Indian Affairs. He had a good deal of experience serving both and, as he saw it, the Bureau was little

Above: The image of the buckskin-clad Indian fighter endured long after Kit Carson finally hung up his spurs.

more than a bunch of political hacks on the gravy train, pocketing Indian aid money for themselves. Besides, Carson strongly believed that the whites were far from blameless for the current state of affairs, and that only martial law could protect the settlers from the Indians. More importantly, he felt the War Department would also safeguard the Indians "from the reckless injustice of those outlaws of society thronging upon the border, whose criminality has too often been the means of rousing the Indians to thoughts of vengeance, and carrying fire and desolation to many a homestead." Strong words from a celebrated Indian fighter.

As is often the case, it was a long time before Congress digested the committee's report and promulgated a new law making the reservation system its official policy. It noted that "as their hunting grounds were taken away, the reservation system, which is the only alternative to their extermination, must be adopted." Of course, this was all easier said than done, and the committee strongly recommended that Kit Carson should be appointed to make peace with the various tribes involved. In the midst of his new career as a peace-maker, Carson assumed command of Fort Union, the major military outpost in New Mexico, and was promoted to Brigadier General. His last important act was accompanying the chiefs of the Ute nation to Washington to witness President Andrew Johnson's signing of a peace treaty, which granted them sovereignty over the western slope of the mountains of Colorado. Much of this same territory had once been the domain of the mountain men.

But Kit Carson knew that he was one of the last of that breed of men. His health was failing and he was near death at the time. The doctors of the time knew that he was suffering from a ballooning blood vessel in his chest called an aneurysm; but while they could diagnose the condition, there wasn't a thing they could do about it. They also knew that it had probably been caused by high blood pressure, but considering the diet of the average mountain man, that wouldn't have been unusual. Kit Carson died, not so peacefully, in bed in late May of 1868. Out of the flood of obituaries that were published across the country, one that appeared in a Salt Lake City newspaper may have summed up the old Indian fighter's reputation best, at least to the new settlers of the West: "To the red man, he was the voice of fate," it read. "To them, he was the voice crying the coming of a race against which they could not prevail, before which they were to be swept away."

General Phil Sheridan remembered him as "... a good type of the class of men most useful in their day, but now as antiquated as Jason of the Golden Fleece, Ulysses of Troy, the Chevalier La Salle of the Lakes, Daniel Boone of Kentucky, Jim Bridger, and Jim Beckwourth of the Rockies; all belonging to a dead past."

Left: Kit Carson in the flesh hardly lived up to the legend. General Sherman described him as "a stoop–shouldered man with reddish hair, freckled face, soft blue eyes and nothing to indicate extraordinary courage and daring."

That, of course, was only one man's opinion. General Sheridan would go on to mastermind the Indian Wars that followed on the Great Plains; if he had taken a lesson from the dead past of the mountain men, it may well have been less costly on both sides. When Sheridan was sent west to solve the Indian problem, he announced that he planned to attack them during the winter, believing that their horses and warriors would be weak and malnourished during those cold months.

Below: Mountain men re-enactment is a fast growing phenomenon. Here, two re-enactors set up their camp near Pinedale, Wyoming.

Jim Bridger knew better and took it upon himself to ride out to Fort Hayes in Kansas, Sheridan's headquarters, to warn the General that the winter would be just as hard on his men as it would be on the Indians, and that he was making a mistake. But Old Gabe was a figure out of what the general considered "the dead past." He listened to what the mountain man had to tell him, but he wouldn't change his mind. In fact, Sheridan argued that a single short, swift campaign using his better-fed troops would be enough to end the conflict.

General Sheridan was at the head of the main column when they marched out in the middle of November. But during their first night in the field, a blizzard stopped them dead in their tracks. Their tents were blown down, and the soldiers were unable to set them back up in the face of sixty mile-an-hour gale-force winds. Sheridan confided in his diary that, "[s]hivering from the wet and cold, I took refuge under a wagon, and there spent such a miserable night that, when at last morning came, the gloomy predictions of Old Man Bridger and others rose up before me with greatly increased force."

Such was the legacy of the mountain men. Some took it to heart, others did not. Those who did discovered for themselves that these men had been much more than just itinerant beaver trappers.

Above: Father De Smet's monument near Pinedale, Wyoming. He was a Catholic missionary who traveled the mountains and wrote about his experiences in his book *Oregon Missions and Travels over the Rocky Mountains.*